What Do You Think of That!

A Collection of Devotional Thought Starters

Compiled by
Joel Lewis

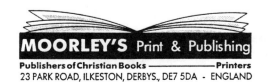

MOORLEY'S Print & Publishing

Publishers of Christian Books ———— **Printers**
23 PARK ROAD, ILKESTON, DERBYS., DE7 5DA - ENGLAND

ISBN 0 86071 385 7

Foreword

Over the years I have collected sayings, facts and figures, proverbs and the like, linking each with a portion of Scripture. Where I have known the source or author I have included that information.

Thinking it would be good to share them with others, I approached the editor of our local free paper. Mr. A. Crocker, the editor of the Herald & Post (which has a weekly distribution of 49,220) agreed to put them in on a weekly basis. I have now put them all together to make this book.

There is a thought for each day of the year; and there are many illustrations that a preacher could place in a sermon, thus giving a window to let light shine on his subject matter.

I am indebted to my wife, Pauline, for her encouragement and the assistance given in checking my notes. And I trust that this book will bring a breathe of refreshment to your soul.

R.J.Joel Lewis, B.A., B.Th.

The word "Selah" is found 71 times in the Psalms and 3 times in Habakkuk. Many and varied have been its interpretation. The Amplified Translation has, "Pause, and calmly think of that."
Hence my title: "What do you think of that!"

1. Colonel Ingersoll, an American agnostic, standing by the grave of his brother, said, "Life is a narrow vale, between the peaks of two Eternities. We strive in vain to look beyond the heights. We cry aloud, and the only answer is the echo of our wailings."

   What a contrast is the comfort of God's Word to that of the agnostic:

   1 Thessalonians 4:13-17, *"But I do not want you to be ignorant, brethren, concerning those who have fallen asleep, lest you should sorrow as others who have no hope. For if we believe that Jesus died and rose again, even so God will bring with Him those who sleep in Jesus...The dead in Christ will rise first, then we who are alive and remain...we shall always be with the Lord."*

2. A sundial was being erected in one of the large gardens in London. Fred was sent to the local library to ask for a suitable inscription.

   Arriving at the library he knocked on the office door. Receiving no reply he turned the handle and entered inside and found the librarian asleep.

   The boy shouted in the librarian's ear, "Please sir, I've come for the motto for the sundial."

   The man awoke with a start, glared fiercely at the boy and shouted, "Begone about your business."

   "Thank you, sir," replied the boy, and went off to deliver the motto, which was later written on the dial!

   Jesus said to His parents, *"Wist ye not that I must be about My Father's business?"* (Luke 2:49).

3. Some young lads were kicking a ball about in a school yard. They seemed to be having a most enjoyable time. That is, with the exception of two lads standing by looking rather glum, seemingly just watching. Near by was one of the school teachers who had been watching them play for some time. He went up to the two lads and asked, "Why aren't you playing with the others?"

   They replied, "We can't sir, we're the goalposts!"
   The apostle Paul writes, *"Not that I speak in regards to need, for I have learned in whatever state I am, to be content."* (Philippians 4:11).

4. Palm Sunday: Something like 1,500 species of palms are known; they are evergreen. Roman gladiators, victorious in a fight, were awarded palm leaves - a coveted prize. So the branches of a palm became a symbol of triumph, victory, pre-eminence, success.

When Jesus rode on an ass into Jerusalem, the crowds strewed before Him leaves of a date palm.

Psalm 24:10, *"Who is (He then), this King of glory? The Lord of Hosts, He is the King of glory. Selah (pause and think on that!)"*.

5. "Easter" comes from the Anglo-Saxon "Eastre", the dawn goddess, or goddess of light and spring. It is Springtime, when new growth is starting. Lambs are born and birds are nesting.

   Easter marks the dawn of a new year, the end of the reign of winter and the advent of increasing light and heat.

   It was at this time that Christ was crucified, and on the third day He arose from death. This gives a new meaning to Easter.

   Song of Solomon 2:11, *"For lo, the winter is past, the rain is over and gone, the flowers appear on the earth, the time of the singing of birds is come..."*

6. "A miracle is an event with which human comprehension has not yet caught up. It is not an interpretation of law, but the working of a law which human reason has not yet charted." (Ralph W. Sockman).

   Acts 15:12, *"Then the multitude kept silent as they listened to Barnabas and Paul declaring how many miracles and wonders God had worked through them among the Gentiles."*

7. Sitting at the breakfast table, a little girl saw a ray of sunshine on the table top. As she lifted a spoonful of cereal to her mouth the sun shone on it.

   "Mammy", she cried, "I have swallowed a spoonful of sunshine."

   Jesus said, *"I am the light of the world."* (John 8:12). He can fill your day with sunshine.

8. A young college student in need of cash sent a short telegram home: "Dear Dad, no mon, no fun, your son."
   Father wrote back on three large sheets the words: "How sad. Too bad. Your Dad." The boy got the message!

   The apostle Peter when in trouble uttered a short prayer that covered all the essentials: *"Lord, save me!"* (Matthew 14:30).

9. Clouds are the handwriting of the weather. I understand that there are ten main types of clouds, and each carries its own message about the weather to come.

    Listen to what the good old book has to say:

    Jesus said to the multitudes, *"When you see a cloud rising out of the west, immediately you say, ' a shower is coming'; and so it is. And when you see the south wind blow, you say, 'There will be hot weather'; and there is. Ye hypocrites! You can discern the face of the sky and of the earth, but how is it you do not discern this time?"* (Luke 12:54-56).

10. An old weather beaten fisherman took a young college student out in his boat on the sea. The student was trying to impress the old gent with all that he had learned about philosophy, psychology, biology and theology.

    Suddenly the student saw water seeping into the boat. The fisherman said, "I know little about your "ologies" but do you know anything about "swimology"?

    2 Timothy 1:12, *"..for I know whom I have believed, and am persuaded that He is able to keep that which I have committed unto Him against that day."*

11. Charles Kingsley wrote:
    "Do the work that's nearest, though it's dull at whiles, Helping, when we meet them, lame dogs over stiles."

    We can hold out a helping hand, give assistance to one in distress, or encourage someone along the way.

    Jesus said, *"In as much as you have done it unto one of the least of these my brethren, you have done it unto me."* Matthew 25:40.

12. A Christian farmer fixed a weather vane on his house, with the text - "God is love" pointing the way of the wind. A friend asked him if the text so placed indicated that the love of God was as changeable as the wind.

    "No," said the farmer, "it means that 'God is love' at all times, at all seasons, no matter how the wind blows."

    Jeremiah 31:3 reads, *"The Lord has appeared of old to me saying, Yes, I have loved you with an everlasting love: therefore with loving kindness have I drawn you."*

13. While on holiday in North Wales, I visited the grave of the faithful hound, Gelert.

    The story goes that the dog had not followed his master as usual, and when the chieftain returned from hunting, the dog greeted him, blood dripping from his jowls.

Fearing the worst, he rushed to the cradle of his infant son to find it empty, and all around the sight of affray. He slew the dog, only to find to his lasting sorrow, that the baby was alive, the dog having risked his life to save it from a fierce wolf.

No wonder his master wanted his faithfulness remembered.

How much more should we remember Christ? *"The Son of God Who loved me and gave Himself for me."* Galatians 2:20.

14. While no formal list exists of the "Seven wonders of the Modern World", the Reader's Digest editors selected the following:
    1. The Taj Mahal. 2. The Great Wall of China. 3. The Easter Island statues. 4. The Eiffel Tower. 5. The Mayan city of Tikal, Central America. 6. The space shuttle (Columbia). 7. Chartres Cathedral.

    A greater wonder still:

    The Psalmist (Psalm 139:14 wrote, *"I will praise Thee; for I am fearfully and wonderfully made: marvellous are Thy works; and that my soul knoweth right well."*

15. Notice on a bus - "Mind your head when rising".

    "..everyone who exalts himself will be abased, and he who humbles himself will be exalted." (Luke 18:14).

16. Did you know that it takes only six volts to make your door bell ring, but 230 volts to light the electric bulb in your lounge? In other words, it is easy to make a lot of noise, but not so easy to let your light shine.

    Jesus said, *"Let your light so shine before men that they may see your good works, and glorify your Father which is in heaven."* Matthew 5:16.

17. In my reading I found these words by Julia A.Carney:
    "Little drops of water,
       Little grains of sand,
    Make a mighty ocean
       And the beauteous land.

    And the little moments,
       Humble though they be,
    Make the mighty ages
       Of eternity."

Take a few minutes and read Proverbs 30:24-28.

18. One little fellow prayed, "Lord, if you can't make me a better boy, don't worry about it. I'm having a real good time as it is."

    Proverbs 20:17 says, *"Bread of deceit is sweet to a man: but afterwards his mouth shall be filled with gravel."*

19. "Smiles" is the longest word in the dictionary, for between the two "s's" we have a "mile!"

    > "Smile awhile, and when you smile, another smiles
    > And soon there's miles and miles of smiles
    > And life's worthwhile - because you smile!"

    Psalm 51:8, *"Make me to hear joy and gladness, that the bones which you have broken may rejoice."*

20. The Sunday School teacher was giving a lesson on love to a class of small children. Then she asked the question, "Why does God love us all so much?"

    One little hand shot up, "Yes?" asked the teacher, and wee Lyn replied, "Because, Miss, God has only one of each of us!"

    Matthew 18:11, *"Take heed that you do not despise one of these little ones, for I say to you that in heaven their angels always see the face of my Father Who is in heaven."*

21. It is not the hours you put in, but what you put in the hours that count.

    Romans 12:11, *"Never lag in zeal and in earnest endeavour; be aglow and burning with the Spirit, serving the Lord."*

22. A little girl and her brother were on their way to visit grandmother. They were carrying a basket of delicious cakes covered with a cloth to keep off the flies.

    Mary lifted the cloth just to have one last look at the cakes, her mouth watering to taste them.

    While gazing at the cakes and on the point of taking one, the little girl looked up into the face of her brother and asked, "Can God count?"

    This settled the matter and grandmother got all her cakes!

    "The eyes of the Lord are in every place, keeping watch upon the evil and the good." (Proverbs 15:3).

23.   "One ship drives East
                 One ship drives West
                 By the selfsame wind that blows.
                 Its not the gale
                 But the set of the sail
                 While determines the way its goes."

"Set your heart and your soul to seek the Lord."

(1 Chronicles 22:19).

24.   A story is told by Dr.W.Graham Scroggie of a boy who received on his birthday three gifts. A box of chocolates, a silver watch and a beautiful Bible. Sometime later the boy was asked what had become of his birthday gifts. He replied, "The box of chocolates - well! It's gone. The silver watch is going. But the Bible is the Word of God and it endures for ever." (1 Pet.1:25).

25.   A teacher in a Sunday School class asked her children: "Who can tell me what a yoke is?" One smart lassie replied: "It is something they put on the neck of animals."

"Now then," said the teacher, "can you tell me what is the meaning of God's yoke?

"After a short pause, a young lad slowly put up his hand and said: "It is God putting his arms around our necks.

"Matthew 11:30, *"For My yoke is easy, and my burden is light."*

26.   Children seldom misquote you; they repeat word for word what you SHOULD NOT have said!

Deut.11:18-19, *"Therefore you shall lay up these My words in (mind and) heart.. And you shall teach them to your children, speaking of them when you sit in your house, and when you walk along the road, when you lie down and when you rise up."*

27.   "When you are looking for faults to correct,look in the mirror!" (Anon). Luke 6:41, *"And why do you look at the speck in your brother's eye, but do not perceive the plank in your own eye?"*

28.   Did you know that David, the psalmist, had two sheep dogs? You will find their names in Psalm 23. They are "Goodness" and "Mercy". Psalm 23:6, *"Surely GOODNESS and MERCY shall follow me all the days of my life.."*

29. A mother was telling her son the story of Jesus Christ. When she had finished talking she asked her son, "What if Jesus came into this room? What would you do?"

He replied, "I would take the Bible and give it to Him and say, "Jesus, This is your Life!"
"And beginning at Moses and all the prophets, He expounded unto them in all the scriptures the things concerning Himself (Jesus)."
(Luke 24:27).

30. A father told his son who was always getting into trouble, "Each day you do something bad I'll knock a nail into this board." Within two weeks there were fourteen nails in the board.

His father then said, "For each day you are good I will take one nail out." Soon there were no nails on the board, but the marks of the nails remained!

But God's Word says, *"...I will forgive their iniquity, and I will remember their sin no more."* (Jer.31:34).

31. "Influenza" is an Italian word for influence. We've all got "influenza"! Stand in a crowded street and keep looking up at a roof-top, soon you will have others looking! Whistle a well-known tune and others will join in.

Influence is something that flows out of our lives into the lives of those around us making them stronger or weaker.

Of the Christian it should be said, *"You are the salt of the earth."* (Matthew 5:13).

32. You may recall the seven wonders of the ancient world:
1. The Pharos Lighthouse at Alexandria. 2. The Statue of Jupiter in Athens. 3. The Hanging Gardens of Babylon. 4. The great Pyramid. 5. The Holicarnassus (Mausoleum). 6. The Colossus of Rhodes (over-thrown by an earthquake). 7. The Temple of Diana in Ephesus.
But of God it can be said: *"How Great are His signs! His kingdom is an everlasting kingdom, and His dominion is from generation to generation"* (Daniel 4:3).

33. A little lad was taking part in a Christmas play. He was heard to recite a piece concerning the three wise men. As he did so he referred to their gifts as, "gold, frankincense and ME."

"This is the greatest gift that you can give to Christ Who gave all for you." (see Romans 12:1).

34.	Here is something to think about: "Hardening of the heart ages people more quickly than hardening of the arteries!"

"So, keep thy heart with all diligence; for out of it are the issues of life". (Proverbs 4:23).

35.	A lay-preacher took his son along to the little church where he was to conduct the service. As they entered the porch the lad noticed a box marked "Free-will offering".

He asked his dad to put something in and he did so, a fifty pence piece. After the service he was handed the contents of the box - fifty pence.

On the way home the little fellow looked up and said: "Dad, if you had put more in, you would have had more out!

"2 Cor. 9:6, *"..he which soweth sparingly shall reap also sparingly; and he which soweth bountifully shall reap also bountifully."*

36.	Years ago in London, a sceptic in speaking of the Bible remarked, "It is quite impossible in these days to believe in any book whose authority is unknown".

In the gathering was a Christian who asked if the compiler of the multiplication table was known. The reply was "No!"

"Then, of course," said the Christian, "you do not believe it." "Oh yes" replied the sceptic, "I believe it because it works well."

"So does the Bible," said the Christian. To this the sceptic had no answer.

Proverbs 6:23, *"For the commandment is a lamp, and the whole teaching of the law is light, and reproofs of discipline are the ways of life."*

37.	Dr. Billy Graham once wrote:
"We are the Bibles the world is reading: We are the creeds the world is needing: We are the sermons the world is heeding."
1	Peter 2:12 (Amp.) *"Conduct yourselves properly (honourably, righteously) among the Gentiles, so that although they may slander you as evil doers, (yet) they may by witnessing your good deeds (come to) glorify God in the day of inspection [when God shall look upon (you) wanderers, as a pastor (shepherd) over his flock]."*

38.	A little boy returning home from a church service with his mother stopped at the gate while his mother went into the house.

Later, looking out of the window the mother saw her son kneeling in the garden. When he came in she asked him what he had been doing.

He replied, "I just wanted to give God a chance. You see," he said, "in the service the minister was praying telling God to do this and do that, bless somebody, forgive somebody else, and I thought God must be tired of being bossed so much, so I went into the garden and said, "God, if there is anything you would like to say to me, I am ready to listen."

Revelation 2:7, *"Let anyone who has an ear listen.."*

39. Of the sea it has been said, "The more you drink of it, the more thirsty you are." This is true of other things in life. The more land you possess, the more you want. The more money you have, the more you desire.

    Jesus said to the woman by the wayside well, *"Whoever drinks this water"* pointing to Jacob's well, *"will be thirsty again, but whoever drinks the water that I will give him will never be thirsty again..."* (John 4:13-14).

40. It was on a journey across the mountains of New Guinea that my wife learned a lesson that has helped her in many a hard situation. No, she didn't have the strength to climb the two mountains that she knew lay between her and home. But! she did have strength for the next step!

    "As your days, so shall your strength be." (Deut.33:25). Remember - Each day is made up of moments.

41. As a young man I worked in Newlands colliery with an Irish electrician. I will always remember the words Paddy taught me.
    "Consider carefully thy words,
        As them you never can recall.
    For when you pull the trigger
        It's too late to stop the ball."
    The Bible records the prayer of David, *"Set a guard, O Lord, before my mouth; keep watch at the door of my lips."* (Psalm 141:3).

42. The Christian should be thankful for the many translations of the Bible. But is it not true: The Bible does not need to be rewritten - it needs to be re-read!

    Nehemiah 8:8, *"So they read from the book of the law of God, distinctly, faithfully amplifying and giving the sense, so that (the people) understood the reading."*

43. Gladys, age seven, was having supper in the kitchen when mummy heard a dramatic crash.

    "Gladys, have you broken that plate?" called out her mother sternly.

    "Only a wee bit of it, Mummy," comes the timely reply.

    James 2:10, *"For whoever shall keep the whole law, and yet stumble in one point, he is guilty of all."*

44. Ralph Emerson wrote: "The only way to have a friend is to be one."

    Proverbs 17:17, *"A friend loves at all times, and a brother is born for adversity."*

45. These words were written on a tombstone:

    "Robert Lewis esq. A barrister, so great a lover of peace that when a contention arose between living and death he immediately yielded up the ghost."

    But Paul says to Timothy: *"FIGHT the good fight of faith, lay hold on eternal life, ..."* (1 Timothy 6:12).

46. Simeon was asked, "What is conscience?" He replied, "Conscience is something that makes you tell your mother before your sister does!"

    John 8:9, *"Then those who heard it, being convicted by their conscience, went out one by one, beginning with the oldest even to the last. And Jesus was left alone, and the woman standing in the midst."*

47. A young lad with his father was taken on a tour round an ancient church. The father was trying to explain to his son what a saint was. Together they gazed up at one depicted in a stained glass window.

    The lad did not seem to show any interest until suddenly the sun shone through the window, making it alive.
    "Oh, now I see," exclaimed the lad, " a saint is someone the sun shines through."

    Stephen was a saint, who when the crowd was about to stone him said, *"Look! I see the heavens opened and the Son of Man standing at the right hand of God!"* (Acts 7:56).

48. Says A.R.Adams, "Don't stay away from church because there are so many hypocrites. There's always room for one more."

    Matthew 7:5, *"Hypocrite! First remove the plank from your own eye, and then you will see clearly to remove the speck from your brother's eye."*

49. The story has been told in various forms of Albert Drecker who having left his box to close the drawbridge over the Passaic River for a train to cross, his little boy of ten, came running after him, and fell into the river.

    A scream from the child reached his father's ears, just as he was closing the bridge, and the train was in view dashing along.

    To leave the bridge would involve the loss of many lives. To stand at his post would sacrifice the life of his boy.

    He remained at his post, the train passed over in safety, but when he turned to look for his child he had sunk. It was only his duty, but it was bravely done. He sacrificed his son whom he loved to save the train and its passengers. It was the limit of human love.

    Romans 5:6-8, "...*But God demonstrates His own love towards us, in that while we were still sinners, Christ died for us.*"

50. A wee fellow feeling rather lonely, said to his mother, "Mummy, I wish I were two little puppies so that I could play together."

    Hebrews 13:5, "....*I will never leave you nor forsake you.*"

51. Consider this riddle, "Used often, it won't wear out. Don't be afraid to give yours to someone without one, you'll probably get it right back."

    Psalm 126:2, "*Then our mouth was filled with laughter, and our tongue with singing..*"

52. It has been said, "Swallowing your pride will never give you indigestion."

    Proverbs 16:19, "*Better to be of a humble spirit with the lowly, than to divide the spoil with the proud.*"

53.   Sow a thought, you reap an action;
          Sow an action, you reap a habit:
          Sow a habit, you reap a character:
          Sow a character, you reap a destiny.

    2 Corinthians 10:5, "*Casting down arguments and every high thing that exalts itself against the knowledge of God, bringing every thought into captivity to the obedience of Christ.*"

54. Says J.N.Darby, "God's ways are behind the scenes, and He moves all the scenes He is behind."

Psalm 77:13-19, "Your way, O God, is in the sanctuary; Who is so great a God as our God....Your way was in the sea, your path in the great waters."

55.   A sundial in Spain has this appropriate motto engraved on it: "I mark only the bright hours."

Paul, the apostle, wrote, *"For it is God who commanded light to shine out of darkness Who has shone in our hearts to give the light of the knowledge of the glory of God in the face of Jesus Christ."* (2 Corinthians 4:6).

56.   It has been said, "Talk may be cheap, but we often pay dearly for it."

Colossians 4:6, *"Let your speech always be with grace, seasoned with salt, that you may know how you ought to answer each other."*

57.   When the lips slip:

> "If you your lips would keep from slips,
> Five things observe with care-
> Of whom you speak, to whom you speak,
> And how, and when, and where."

Proverbs 14:3, *"In the mouth of a fool is a rod of pride, but the lips of the wise will preserve them."*

58.   A farmer warning trespassers of his bull, had a wry sense of humour. He put this notice on the gate into the field:

> "ENTRANCE FREE. CHARGE LATER."

So it is with sin. But of Moses it is said: *"Choosing rather to suffer affliction with the people of God, than to enjoy the pleasure of sin for a season..for he fixed his gaze on the coming reward."* (Hebrews 11:25-26).

59.   A friend of mine once told the story of a little boy in an orphanage who was recovering from an illness. He saw an advertisement, "Fry's Cocoa - Absolutely pure."

When he asked the nurse what "absolutely pure" meant, he was told - "pure all through, nothing bad in it and all the nasty things taken out."

That evening the nurse was surprised to hear the lad pray - "O Lord make me like Fry's Cocoa." She was shocked, and was about to interrupt when the lad continued - "Like Fry's Cocoa, absolutely pure, so there will be nothing bad in me at all, for Jesus's sake. Amen." (Matt.5:8).

60. I saw these words the other day: "If you think education is expensive, try ignorance."

   2 Timothy 2:15, *"Study and be eager and do your utmost to present yourself to God approved (tested by trial), a workman who has no cause to be ashamed, correctly analysing and accurately dividing - rightly handling and skilfully teaching - the word of God."*

61. S.J.Miller, a doctor I met in Rhodesia (now Zimbabwe) said, "Peace does not come in capsules." This is regrettable, because medical science recognizes that emotions such as fear, sorrow, envy, resentment and hatred are responsible for much sickness.

   No, not in capsules, but we can have peace, as Dr. Miller would agree. Jesus said, *"Peace I leave with you. My peace I give, let not your heart be troubled, neither let it be afraid."* (John 14:27).

62. Before you start:- "Be sure your brain is running before you put your tongue in gear"

   Ephesians 4:29, *"Let no corrupt communication proceed out of your mouth, but what is good for necessary edification, that it may impart grace to the hearers."*

63. The story is told of a converted drunkard who said, "Lord, we ain't what we want to be, we ain't what we ought to be, and we ain't what we're gonna be - but we thank thee, Lord, we ain't what we used to be!"

   The man who was born blind and received his sight through Jesus said, *"...One thing I know: that though I was blind, now I see."* (John 9:25).

64. "A wise man sees an opportunity in difficulty; a fool sees difficulty in an opportunity."

   Galatians 6:10, *"Therefore as we have opportunity, let us do good to all, especially to those who are of the household of faith."*

65. The teacher of a class of boys asked the question, "Can any of you tell me one thing of great importance that we have now which we did not have a hundred and sixty years ago?"
   Naturally he was expecting answers such as, 'an aeroplane, radio, cars, robots, computers'.
   One bright lad in the class put up his hand, "I know, sir" he replied.
   "Well," said the teacher, "what is it?"
   "Why - ME, sir!" How true!!

   Jeremiah 31:3, *"The Lord has appeared of old to me, saying: 'Yes, I have loved you with an everlasting love; therefore with loving-kindness I have drawn you."*

66. It is better to bite your tongue than to let it bite someone else."

"Where there is no wood, the fire goes out; and where there is no tale-bearer, strife ceases." (Proverbs 26:20)

67. Weigh this up! I quote the words of W.A.Ward,
"Though the human tongue weighs practically nothing, it is surprising how few people are able to hold it!"

"Whoever guards his mouth and tongue keeps his soul from troubles." (Prov.21:23).

68. These few words tell us a lot: "The Bible will keep you from sin - or sin will keep you from the Bible."

"Your word I have hidden in my heart, that I might not sin against You." (Psalm 119:11).

69. Give these words serious consideration: "Discontent makes rich men poor, while contentment makes poor men rich!"

The apostle Paul wrote, *"Not that I speak in regard to need, for I have learned in whatever state I am, to be content."* (Phil.4:11).

70. The following notice was seen at a bank:
Yesterday is a cancelled cheque.
Tomorrow is a promissory note.
Today is ready cash - use it!

"Today, if you will hear His voice, do not harden your hearts.." (Hebrews 3:7-8).

71. How true is the statement, "A church without children is like a smile without teeth."

Jesus said, *"...Let the little children come to Me, and do not forbid them; for of such is the kingdom of God."* (Matthew 19:14).

72. A shoe firm hoping to increase their business sent two sales men up the Amazon to cover different areas.

One sent a telegram - "Returning home on next plane. Impossible to sell shoes here; everyone goes barefooted."

The other sales man sent a telegram, "Sales booming and prospects unlimited; nobody has shoes here!"

In Numbers 13, ten of the twelve spies sent into Canaan came back with a bad report, but two with a good one.

73. Robert Louis Stevenson as a young lad once sat by a window at eventide. Looking out of the window he could see the lamp-lighter lighting the lamps of the city.

His mother came to his side and asked him, "What are you doing?"

He replied, "I am watching a man punch holes in the darkness."

Jesus said, *"I am the light of the world: he that followeth Me shall not walk in darkness but shall have the light of life."*   John 8:12.

74. A little boy and his sister were staying with their parents at a hotel until a house could be found.

A dear old lady said to Willie, "I am sorry you do not have a home."

Willie replied, "Oh, we have a home, we just don't have a house to put it in."

Psalm 68:6, *"God places the solitary in families and gives the desolate a home in which to dwell."*

75. In northern Italy there is the Leaning Tower of Pisa. It was built as a bell tower for the nearby cathedral. Its top is about 17 feet out of true because the tower's foundations are inadequate; only 10 feet deep. The tower itself is 179 feet high and weighs 14,453 tons.

Back in 1173, almost as soon as building began, the tower started to settle sideways, it was not completed for nearly 200 years.

Jesus said: *"Whosoever cometh to Me, and heareth My sayings, and doeth them, I will shew you to who he is like: He is like a man which built a house, and digged deep, and laid foundation on a rock: and when the flood arose, the stream beat vehemently upon that house, and could not shake it: for it was founded upon a rock."* (Matthew 7:24-25).

76. Listen! "There is no one so deaf as the person who refuses to hear."

Jeremiah 5:21, *"Hear this now, O foolish people, without understanding, who have eyes and see not, and who have ears and hear not."*

77. An unknown person wrote, "The youth who stands with a glass of liquor in his hand would do well to consider which he had best throw away, the liquor or himself."

Proverbs 20:1 reads, *"Wine is a mocker, strong drink a riotous brawler, and whoever errs or reels because of it is not wise."*

78. You may have heard the story of the five blind men who each described an elephant.

One felt the trunk and said it was like a pipe. One felt the foot and said it was like a trunk of a tree. Another grabbed the tail and described it as a rope. The fourth touched its tusk and said it was like a stake, and the fifth bumped into it and thought it was a wall!

1 Corinthians 13:12, *"For now we see through a glass darkly; but then face to face; now I know in part; but then shall I know even as also I am known."*

79. Here is a quote from Beech: "I can forgive, but I can't forget." is another way of saying, "I cannot forgive!"

Writes the apostle Paul, *"And you, being dead in your trespasses...He has made alive....having forgiven you all trespasses...He has taken it out of the way, having nailed it to the cross."* (Colossians 2:13-14).

80.   "Could we with ink the ocean fill,
            And were the sky of parchment made,
        Were every blade of grass a quill,
            And every man a scribe by trade;
        To write the love of God above,
            Would drain the ocean dry;
        Nor would the scroll contain the whole,
            Tho' stretched from sky to sky."

Romans 5:8, *"But God demonstrates His own love towards us, in that while we were still sinners, Christ died for us."*

81. A church notice read: "Work for the Lord. The pay isn't much, but the retirement plan is out of this world!"

Jesus said, *"Let not your heart be troubled: ye believe in God, believe also in Me. In My Father's house are many mansions (abiding places).."* John 14:1-2.

82. In my reading I came across these words:
        "If you plant for a year, plant grain.
        If you plant for ten years, plant trees.
        If you plant for 100 years, plant men.
        If you plant for eternity, plant the Word."

The Bible contains the mysterious principle which we call the "life principle". *"He who goes forth bearing precious seeds, and weeps (because he has to use his precious supply of grain for sowing), shall doubtless come again rejoicing, bringing his sheaves with him."* Psa 126:6.

83. Think on these words: "Christianity begins where religion ends - with the resurrection."
1 Corinthians 15:20, "But now Christ has risen from the dead, and has become the first-fruits of those who have fallen asleep."

84. I was living for a time in the north-east of Scotland. Walking down the street in one of the towns I saw a notice in a hair-dressers shop: You must dye sometime, so why not dye now?

    Hebrews 9:27, *"And just as it is appointed for (all) men once to die and after that the (certain) judgment."*

85. A Chinese proverb says: "In a field of melons do not stoop to tie your shoe." (Since that will look as if you want to steal the melons!)

    The Bible says, *"Abstain from all appearance of evil."* 1 Thes.5:22.

86. Don't just count the days, make the days count; for "lost time" is never "found" again!

    1 Corinthians 7:29, *"But this I say, brethren, the time is short, so that from now on even those who have wives should be as though they had none."*

87. Please give this following statement your careful consideration: "Bibles that are coming apart usually belong to people who are not!"

    "If you instruct the brethren in these things, you will be a good minister of Jesus Christ, nourished in the word of faith and of the good doctrine which you have carefully followed." (1 Timothy 4:6).

88. I came across this interesting piece: A minister dreamed that he had been invited to visit heaven. On being shown around by one of the angels he asked.

    "Any Baptist here?" the reply was "No". "Any Roman Catholics, Methodists or Presbyterians?" Again the answer was "No". "Any Pentecostals?" still the answer was "No".

    "What!" said the minister, "Then who have you got up here?"

    The angel answered, "We have only people who loved the Lord" (No labels!).

    "And you shall love the Lord your God with all your heart, with all your soul, with all your mind, and with all your strength.." (Mark 12:30).

89. David Otis Fuller asked the question: "If you were arrested for being a Christian, would there be enough evidence to convict you?"

    Jesus said, *"Let your light so shine before men that they may see your moral excellence and your praiseworthy, noble and good deeds, and recognize and honour and praise and glorify your Father Who is in heaven."* (Matthew 5:16, Amp.).

90. How true! "Humility is a strange thing - when you think you have it, you haven't!"

    "Likewise you younger people, submit yourselves to your elders. Yes, all of you be submissive to one another, and be clothed with humility, for God resists the proud, but gives grace to the humble." (1 Peter 5:5).

91. A mother found someone had been taking pieces from her newly baked bread. She wanted to know which of her three children was the culprit.

    The eldest child was very virtuous and declared, "God saw who did it." But Johnny, the youngest, was indignant, "No, He never, 'cos I shut the door!"

    Jesus said, *"..for there is nothing covered that shall not be revealed, and hid that shall not be known."* (Matt.10:26).

92. Astronomers agree that there is an open space in Orion which is perhaps more than, 16,740,000,000,000 miles in diameter, that is 90,000 times as wide as the diameter of the earth's orbit.

    This was discovered in comparatively recent times. But many thousands of years ago Job said, *"He (God) it is Who spreads out the northern skies over emptiness and hangs the earth upon or over nothing."* (Job.26:7).

93. A Christian farmer, invited to tea by the local squire and his wife, bowed his head and silently thanked God for his meal. The squire, who was not a Christian, derided him, "Nobody does that these days," he said, "it's out of fashion

    "Well, squire," replied the farmer, "as a matter of fact I do have those over on the farm who never say grace at all"

    "Quite right," answered the squire, "who are they?". "The pigs" was the reply!

    "At all times and for everything giving thanks in the name of our Lord Jesus Christ to God the Father." (Ephesians 5:20). And remember, it is not old fashioned to eat!

94. These few words tell us a lot: "The Bible will keep you from sin - or sin will keep you from the Bible."

    "Your Word I have hidden in my heart, that I might not sin against You." (Psalm 119:11).

95. Evan Roberts the revivalist said, "The object of the night is not to reveal the stars, but the work of the stars is to hide the night."

    Gen.1:16, *"And God made the two great lights, the greater light (the sun) to rule the day, and the lesser light (the moon) to rule the night; He also made the STARS"*

96. What makes the Dead Sea dead? It is because it is all the time receiving, but never giving out. It has been said that "some people give according to their means, and others according to their meanness."

    The apostle Paul tells us that Jesus said, *"It is more blessed - it makes one happier and more to be envied - to give than to receive."*
    (Acts 20:35).

97. A man becomes wise by noticing what happens when he isn't!

    Prov.2:2, *"Making your ear attentive to skilful and godly Wisdom, and inclining and directing your heart and mind to understanding - applying all your powers to the quest of it."*

98. I once read that "a display of temper is like an earthquake. It may only last a few seconds, but the subsequent damage may take years to eradicate."

    James, in the Bible, writes, *"Let everyone be swift to hear, slow to speak, slow to wrath."* (James 1:19).

99. Speaking on "Old Age", Dr. Guthrie wrote, "They say I am growing old..but they are mistaken. The knees are weak, but the knees are not me. The brow is wrinkled, but the brow is not me. This is the house I live in; but I am young - younger than I ever was before."

    Paul, the apostle, wrote, *"For we know that if the tent which is our earthly home is destroyed, we have from God a building, a house not made with hands, eternal in the heavens."* (2 Cor.5:1)

100. If you took a sample of the blood of a cat, a cow, a horse and a camel placed each in a separate container, the experts could tell the difference.

    But, if you took the blood of a Frenchman, a German, a Chinese and an African, they could not!
    Nearly 2,000 years ago it was written in the Bible *"God..hath made of one blood all nations of men."* (Acts 17:26)

101. There is an old saying,
"These things come not back:
The spoken word.
The sped arrow.
Time past.
The neglected opportunity.

"Behold, Now is the accepted time; behold, Now is the day of salvation." (2 Cor.6:2).

102. An Arab saying - "All sunshine makes a desert."

Eccl.7:3, *"Sorrow is better than laughter. For by a sad countenance the heart is made better."*

103. Some ministers had gathered together to discuss what they could to to encourage people to come to church.

An old farmer hearing this was greatly shocked. He said to his wife, "In all the years in farming I've never once heard anybody talk about how to get the animals to come to the feeding racks."

John 21:17, *"He (Jesus) said to him the third time, 'Simon, son of Jonah, do you love Me?' Peter was grieved because He said to him the third time, 'Do you love Me?' And he said to Him, 'Lord, you know all things; You know that I love you.' Jesus said to him, 'Feed My sheep.'"*

104. Here's a thought for today, "Forget yourself for others, and others will not forget you."

Philippians 2:3, *"Let nothing be done through selfish ambition or conceit, but in lowliness of mind let each esteem others better than himself."*

105. These words were found in a Christian magazine:-

"Hold this square to your face and blow on it.
If it turns green, call your doctor.
If it turns brown, see your dentist.
If it turns red, see your banker.
If it turns purple, see a psychiatrist.
If it turns black, make your will.

If it stays the same colour, you're in first class health and there is no reason on earth why you shouldn't be in church next Sunday!"

Hebrews 10:25, *"Not forsaking the assembling of ourselves together, as the manner of some, but exhorting one another, and so much the more as you see the Day approaching."*

106. During a storm, hurricane winds shattered a beautiful stained-glass window. A visitor to the church was shown the box of fragments. He was a famous artist, and out of the fragments made another window even more beautiful than the original.

"Beloved do not think it strange concerning the fiery trial which is to try you, as though some strange thing happened to you; but...."

(1 Peter 4:12-13).

107. Little Jean was out walking with her father one evening. Looking up at the stars, she exclaimed, "Oh, Daddy, if the wrong side of heaven is so beautiful, what must the right side be like!"

"But as it is written: Eye has not seen, nor ear heard, nor have entered into the heart of man the things which God has prepared for those who love Him." (1 Cor.2:9)

108. "A good marriage means falling in love many times - BUT always with the same person."

"Nevertheless let each of you in particular so love his own wife as himself, and let the wife see that she respects her husband." (Ephes.5:33).

109. "One trouble with being an atheist is that you have nobody to talk to when you are alone."
"And the hand of the Lord was there upon me, and He said unto me, arise, go forth into the plain, and I will there talk with thee." (Ezekiel 3:22).

110. A cafe owner could not help overhearing the young lad using the cafe telephone saying, "Is that the company which advertised for a boy a few days ago?....Oh, the job is filled...Does the boy do the work to meet your requirements? ...Thank you, goodbye." and put the receiver down.

The cafe owner said, "Tough luck, you missed out."

"No, answered the lad, "I had the job a few days ago. I was just checking up on myself!"

"Examine yourselves as to whether you are in the faith. Prove yourselves. Do you not know yourselves, that Jesus Christ is in you? - unless indeed you are disqualified." (2 Cor.13:5).

111. Consider these words: "It is never too early to give thanks, because we don't know how soon it will be before it is too late."

"We are bound to thank God always for you, brethren, as it is fitting, because your faith grows exceedingly, and the love of every one of you all abounds towards each other." (2 Thes.1:3).

112. Many years ago when in Nigeria I recall an English Examination. The children were asked to write sentences with the following words in them: train, trains, mind, minds.

One young lad wrote: "The teacher trains the mind, and the driver minds the train."!

Proverbs 22:6 says, *"Train up a child in the way he should go, and when he is old he will not depart from it."*

113. It is said that the American Indians of the Choc Fan tribe, before setting out on an exploit hold up a stuffed owl into the wind. If its feathers became ruffled they would believe that danger lay ahead so turned back.

Of course many things could have caused the feathers to ruffle.

Who or what is your guide? The Psalmist says, *"For this God is our God forever; he will be our guide, even unto death."* (Psalm 48:14).

114. A little girl went shopping with her mother. On the way they met a blind man begging. The child asked her mother for something to place in the beggar's hand. Mother replied, "We are in a hurry, and besides he is none of our business."

That evening the daughter surprised her mother when she got down to prayer: "..and dear Jesus please help the poor man we saw today...Oh, I'm sorry, I forgot he's none of our business."

What a difference: Acts 3:6, *"Then said Peter, Silver and gold have I none; but such as I have give I thee; In the name of Jesus Christ of Nazareth rise up and walk."*

115. Long ago in China a missionary was asked why he had kept on preaching "Jesus". The native wanted to know why he did not preach something else.
The missionary asked him, "What did you have for breakfast?" "Rice", he replied. "What did you have for dinner?" Again the reply, "Rice". "Then what did you have yesterday?" Once more he answered, "Rice" "Why?" "Because it keeps me alive."

"And that is why I preach Jesus each day", said the Missionary. John 6:51 reads, *"I am (said Jesus), the living bread which cometh down from heaven, that a man may eat thereof, and not die."*

116. Someone has rightly said, "SEVEN DAYS without church and Christian fellowship makes ONE WEAK!"

Psalm 84:10, *"For a day in Your courts is better than a thousand (anywhere else); I had rather be a door-keeper and stand at the threshold in the house of God than dwell (at ease) in the tents of wickedness."*

117. Someone said, "So live that when you die even the undertaker will be sorry"

2 Cor.7:15, "And his affection for you is all the greater, as he remembers the deference that you all showed him and recalls how you received him with anxious care."

118. Whitsun or Whit Sunday. It is said that it is so called because those who were newly baptised wore white from Easter to Whitsun, or Pentecost, the time the Holy Spirit came and the whole house was filled.

Alan Redpath tells the story of a woman who held home meetings. Trying to persuade a neighbour to come, she told her, "There were 35 present. The house was full."

Later she told her, "There were 51, the place was full." And again, "There were 62 and the house was full."

"Impossible!" the neighbour cried, but she explained simply, "We took out every stick of furniture and put it in the garden."

Are we willing to make room for the Holy Spirit? The Bible says, *"Be filled (keep on being filled) with the Spirit."* (Ephes.5:18).

119. John Ruskin says, "All that I have taught; everything that I have written; every greatness that has been in any thought of mine, has simply been due to the fact that when I was a child, my mother daily read with me a part of the Bible, and daily made me learn a part of it by heart."
The psalmist says that the person who meditates in the Word of God will be "..like a tree planted by the rivers of water, that bring forth its fruit in its season, whose leaf also shall not wither, and whatever he does shall prosper." (Psalm 1:2-3).

120. Many years ago it was recorded in a local paper that a minister got lost in his sermon. It took him two hours to find his way out!

In 1955 in Lagos, I left my ship, hoping to visit a fellow Welshman. He was not in. I got lost in the market place. Time was running out. It was dark. I walked with my face towards the sea breeze and just made it back to the ship.

You can get lost in a crowd, just as easily as in a sermon. *"The Son of Man came to seek and to save that which was lost."* (Luke 19:10).

121. The story is told of a father who, fearing his son was a wastrel, determined in his will that the son might choose any one item of his estate. All the rest was to be left to his faithful slave and steward.

When informed of this the son asked the lawyer if he would give him 24 hours to think it over. The next day he came back and said: "I'll take the slave!"

Accepting Christ, God *"will give us everything besides!"* (Romans 8:32. Moff.).

122. I have been nearly drowned four times! Once in a swimming pool in London, once getting out of a boat I fell into a swiftly flowing river, and once, when in Durban, South Africa I was carried out towards the sharks' nets. My father wrote that I should keep to the bath!

The time I shall refer to here was in Porthcawl. It happened around the month of June 1944. Five of us young men, the Kenfig Hill Gospel Quintet, went down to Rest Bay for a swim before holding a service near Coney Beach.

We changed and ran for the sea - first in and under.

We had been in for some time, then one by one we made for the shore. Suddenly I realized that I was the only one left in the sea. The sand was slipping from under my feet. I was not much of a swimmer and found I was going further and further out to sea; caught in an under-current.

I shouted "help, help, help!" I had gone down once and was going down the second time. I did not see the green pastures, or the faces of my parents. I only thought how strange it was that I was going to drown when I knew within my heart that God had called me to be a missionary.

I was going down for the third time, with more sea inside me than out, when I realized that my younger brother, David, was at my side. I heard him say under his breath, "I can't do it", then I lost consciousness.

With the help of God he pushed me sideways to the current and eventually got me back to land. He would have gone down with me rather than return to my parents alone.

A doctor near at hand worked on me for one hour. A first-aid man took over the artificial respiration for another ten minutes. He, too, gave up. Then a school-master from the Valleys continued. Another ten minutes and I came to. A week in hospital and I was fit and well again.

I owe a great debt to the unknown doctor, first-aid man and the head-master and especially to my brother, but above all to God for saving me from "Davy Jones'locker".

I did go as a missionary, serving in Nigeria and Rhodesia (now Zimbabwe) for 26 years. Now living in Nottage, Porthcawl I often take a stroll and view the place where my earthly days could have ended.

"This poor man cried out, and the Lord heard him, and saved him .." Psalm 34:6.

123. Little Molly stood up in the pulpit to recite the 23rd Psalm. She had given much time to learning it. Now was the time to stand before the large congregation to recite it. But her courage fled.

After a brief pause, out came the words, "The Lord is my shepherd; I shall not want." There was a long silence.

At last little Molly smiled charmingly and said, "The Lord is my shepherd; I shall not want - and I think that's enough for me."

Psalm 22:26, *"The meek shall eat and be satisfied."*

124. "A good marriage requires determination to be married for good."

Matthew 19:6, *"Wherefore they are no more twain, but one flesh. What therefore God hath joined together, let not man put asunder."*

125. "A little lad came home from school one day and said, "Mam, I'm in class three now!"

His mother was delighted and replied, "You must be very clever Samuel"

Samuel's face fell a little, "Well," he said, "it isn't really that. They're painting class two!"

1 Samuel 16:7, *"...For the Lord seeth not as a man seeth; for man looketh on the outward appearance, but the Lord looketh on the heart."*

126. I read this quote some time ago: "The Bible is the only book whose author is always present when it is read."

2 Timothy 3:16, *"All scripture is given by inspiration of God, and is profitable for doctrine, for reproof, for correction, for instruction in righteousness."*

127. "It's not enough to master the scriptures - you must let them master you."

1 Thessalonians 2:13, *"For this cause also thank we God without ceasing, because, ye received the Word of God...as it is in truth the Word of God, which effectually worketh also in you that believe."*

128. Did you hear the story of the lad who received a 20p and a 50p coin from his dad? Dad said to Willie as he set off for Sunday School. "Put whichever you wish into the collection plate. The other one is for yourself."

When the lad arrived home his dad asked him, "Which coin did you place on the collection plate?"

Willie replied, "At first I was going to put the 50p in. Then, just before the plate came round the Sunday School Superintendent told us that the Bible says that the Lord loveth a cheerful giver."

"Well," said dad. The lad continued, "I knew I'd be much more cheerful if I gave the 20p - so that's what I did!"

2 Corinthians 9:6, *"But this I say: He who sows sparingly will also reap sparingly, and he who sows bountifully will also reap bountifully."*

129. Time for thought: "God's clock is never slow, but ours is often fast."

Psalm 25:5, *"...On You I wait all day long."*

130. The famous author and poet, Lord Byron, who spent his life in pursuit of pleasure, penned these words on his last birthday:

"My days are in the yellow leaf,
The flowers and fruits of life are gone,
The worm, the canker, and the grief,
Are mine alone."

What a different outlook is that of the Psalmist (Psalm 92:12,14,)
"The righteous shall flourish like a palm tree, they shall grow like a cedar in Lebanon. They shall still bear fruit in old age; they shall be fresh and flourishing."

131. "Those who are willing to face the music may someday lead the band."

Proverbs 15:5, *"...he who receives reproof is prudent."*

132. "Too many people stop looking for work when they get a job."

Proverbs 18:9, *"He who is slothful in his work is a brother to him who is a great destroyer."*

133. A famous conductor was once asked which instrument he considered most difficult to play.

He hesitated, then with a smile replied, "A second fiddle. I can usually get a first violinist - but a second fiddle with enthusiasm is difficult to find."

Philippians 2:3, *"Let nothing be done through strife or vain glory; but in lowliness of mind let each esteem others better than themselves."*

134. I read this delightful account of an agent of the Bible society who was translating a well-known portion of scripture in Luke's Gospel.

He was having difficulty in finding a word to correspond with 'joy'.

Observing one of the husky dogs enjoying himself immensely with a bone he wrote down, "There shall be tail-wagging in the presence of God over one sinner that repenteth." Luke 15:7.

135. The story is told of the little boy who didn't know how to say his prayers, or what to say to God, so he just went through the alphabet and then said, "Dear God, you put the letters into words and make them into a prayer."

Romans 8:26, *"Likewise, the Spirit also helpeth our infirmities; for we know not what we should pray.."*

136.
"Said the robin to the sparrow,
'I should really like to know
Why those anxious human beings
Rush about and worry so.'
Said the sparrow to the robin,
'Friend, I think that it must be
That they have no heavenly Father
Such as cares for you and me.'"

Matthew 6:31-33, *"Therefore do not worry, saying 'What shall we eat?' or 'What shall we drink?' or 'What shall we wear?'....Seek first the kingdom of God...and all these things shall be added to you."*

137. "It is not a sin to get angry when you get angry at sin" John 2:15, *"And when he had made a scourge of small cords, He drove them all out of the temple..."*

138. Someone wrote:
"Don't look for the flaws as you go through life,
And even when you find them
It is wise and kind to be somewhat blind,
And look for the virtue behind them.
For the cloudiest night has a hint of light
Somewhere in its shadow hiding;
It is better by far to look for a star
Than the spots on the sun abiding."

Philippians 4:8, *"And now, brothers, as I close this letter let me say this one more thing: Fix your thoughts on what is true and good and right. Think about things that are pure and lovely, and dwell on the fine, good things in others. Think about all you can praise God for and be glad about it."*

139. How true the old saying, "You're not ready to live until you're ready to die."

Acts 21:13, *"Then Paul answered, 'What do you mean by weeping and breaking your heart? For I am ready not only to be bound, but also to die at Jerusalem for the name of the Lord Jesus.'"*

140. Is it not true that a 'tight' driver is much more dangerous than a loose wheel!

Proverbs 23:29-30, *"Who has woe? who has sorrow? Who has contentions? Who has complaints? Who has wounds without cause? Who has redness of eyes? Those who linger long at the wine. Those who go in search of mixed wine."*

141. It is important to note that "What one leaves IN their children should concern parents more than what they leave TO them."

Genesis 25:5, *"Abraham gave all that he had to Isaac."*

142. It is said of the lama that you must put on its loads from behind, for it cannot bear to be put on. And if you speak to it harshly it will shed big tears, lie down and die.

Jesus said, *"Come to Me, all you who labour and are heavy laden, and I will give you rest."* (Matthew 11:28).

143. Sir Francis Bacon once asked the question: "Who taught the ant to bite every grain of corn that she buries in the hill lest it should take root and grow?"

Proverbs 6:6, *"Go to the ant you sluggard! Consider her ways and be wise."*

144. "The longest journey starts with a single step."

Psalm 37:23, *"The steps of a good man are ordered by the Lord, and he delights in his way."*

145. Mrs. Evans hurried to the butcher's just before closing time. She had relations coming for the weekend.

Had the butcher anything left?

He had one chicken left, and weighing it said it would be three pounds.

"Oh, dear," says Mrs. Evans, "I need something much bigger."

The butcher goes to the back of the shop, pumps it up a bit then brought it through again. Weighing it he said, "that will be four pounds."

"Great!" said Mrs. Evans, "I'll take them both."

Matthew 10:26, *"...For there is nothing covered that will not be revealed, and hidden that will not be known."*

146. "Your parents brought you UP; don't let them DOWN."

Proverbs 23:15-24, *"....If your heart is wise...listen to your father who begot you, and do not despise your mother when she is old..."*

147. Someone wrote, "Nature FORMS us, sin DEFORMS us, school INFORMS us, only Christ TRANSFORMS us."

Romans 12:1-2, *"I beseech you therefore, brethren, by the mercies of God, that you present your bodies a living sacrifice, holy, acceptable to God, which is your reasonable service. And do not be CONFORMED to this world, but be TRANSFORMED ..."*

148. It has been said, "Words break no bones, but they do break hearts."

Psalm 52:2, *"Your tongue devises destruction, like a sharp razor, working deceitfully."*

149. The story is told of a famous artist who painted a picture of a winter night scene. The sky was dark and lowering. The trees were dense and thick. The cottage in the midst of the picture was dark and gloomy. The whole picture had a sombre tone.
An observer said to the artist, "What a dreary picture!" The artist dipped his brush into the yellow paint and with one stroke transformed the picture. He put a light in the window, and it became the focal point of the picture.

Jesus said, *"I am the Light of the world; he that followeth Me shall not walk in darkness, but shall have the light of life."* (John 8:12).

150. Someone has described worry as "A little stream of fear trickling through the soul." Faith will dry up this annoying stream.

Psalm 55:22, *"Cast your burden on the Lord, and He shall sustain you; He shall never permit the righteous to be moved."*

151. An old man used to carry a little can of oil with him everywhere he went. If he passed a door which squeaked, he would poor a little oil

on the hinges. He went through life lubricating all hard places, making it easier for all who came after him.

Romans 12:10, *"Be kindly affectionate to one another with brotherly love, in honour giving preference to one another."*

152. Little Arthur, who had hurt his finger, ran to his father and cried, "Daddy, I've hurt my finger." The busy father, on seeing that the injury was slight replied, "I can't do anything about it."

The little fellow turned away with tears in his eyes, and quietly said, "You could have said, Oh!'"

1 Peter 3:8, *"Finally, all of you be of one mind, having compassion for one another; love as brothers, be tender-hearted, be courteous."*

153. A selfish prayer: "Lord, bless me and Joe, Will and Flo, we four, no more, evermore. Amen!!

1 Samuel 12:23, *"Moreover, as for me, far be it from me that I should sin against the Lord in ceasing to pray for YOU: I will teach you the good and the right way."*

154. The Sunday school teacher asked the class if anyone could define the word "promise". One bright lassie put up her hand and answered, "To promise means to keep it in your mind, keep it in your mind, keep it in your mind - until you do it."

Ecclesiastes 5:5, *"It is better not to vow than to vow and not pay."*

155. I saw these words on a wall in a restaurant, "Jesus is the rock and He rolled my blues away."

1 Peter 5:7, *"Casting all your care upon Him, for He cares for you."*

156. Here is an interesting piece that I came across some time ago:

"One step won't get you very far -
You've got to keep on walking.
One word won't tell folks who you are -
You've got to keep on talking.
One foot won't make you very tall -
You've got to keep on growing.
One trip to church won't tell you all -
You've got to keep on going!"

Hebrews 10:25, *"Not forsaking the assembling of ourselves together, as is the manner of some, but exhorting one another, and so much the more as you see the Day approaching."*

157. How sad are the words of Disraeli. Prime Minister of Great Britain, having risen to his position from humble life, said, "Youth is a mistake, Manhood a struggle, Old age a regret."

But how triumphant the words of the apostle Paul who says, *"For me to live is Christ, and to die is gain."* (Phil. 1:21)

158. There is a tombstone in Northern Ireland with this inscription on it:

"Remember, Man, as you pass by,
As you are now, so once was I,
As I am now, so you shall be,
Prepare for death and follow me."

Then underneath someone added two more lines:

"To follow you I'd be content,
If I only knew which way you went!"

The apostle Paul said, *"Imitate me, just as I also imitate Christ."* (1 Cor.11:1).

159. Here are some words full of wisdom:

"I'm careful of the words I say,
I keep them soft and sweet -
I never know from day to day
Which ones I'll have to eat."

Ecclesiastes 5:2, *"Do not be rash with your mouth. And let not your heart utter anything hastily before God. For God is in heaven, and you on earth; therefore let your words be few."*

160. A famous painter, G.F.Watt, had this motto:

"What I spent, I had;
What I saved, I lost;
What I gave, I have."

John 12:25, *"He who loves his life will lose it, and he who hates his life in this world will keep it for eternal life."*

161. A group of children on a visit to London were given tea on the terrace of the house of Commons which enjoys a superb view overlooking the Thames.

The teacher said, "Well, what do you think about this?" For a while there was silence. Then a young lad piped up, "The tea's a bit strong, miss!" Matthew 6:21, *"For where your treasure is, there your heart will be also."*

162. Give careful thought to the following words:
     "Never find fault with the man who limps
     Or stumbles along the road,
     Unless you have worn the shoes he wears,
     Or struggled beneath his load."

     Hebrews 4:15, *"For we do not have a high priest who cannot sympathize with our weaknesses, but was in all points tempted as we are, yet without sin."*

163. How important it is to realize that:

     "God's timetable is not altered by the times."

     2 Peter 3:9, *"The Lord is not slack concerning His promises, as some count slackness, but is long-suffering towards us, not willing that any should perish but that all should come to repentance."*

164. Little Joan heard an appeal for toys to be given to a home for underprivileged children. So she very carefully went through her collection of dolls and toys.

     To her mother's surprise Joan put aside nearly all her best dolls to be sent to the home. The only one she kept was a battered old doll which had an eye missing on one side and an arm on the other.

     When asked for an explanation, the little girl came up with the unanswerable reply: "Nobody else would love a poor little thing like this."

     Isaiah 49:15, *"Can a woman forget her nursing child, and not have compassion on the son of her womb? Surely they may forget, yet I will not forget you."*

165. Consider, "Patience is a virtue that carries a lot of wait."

     Proverbs 13:12, *"Hope deferred makes the heart sick, but when the desire comes, it is a tree of life."*

166. Have you ever heard the Fisherman's Prayer?
     "God grant that I may live to fish
     Until my dying days,
     And when it come to my last cast,
     I then most humbly pray,
     When in the Lord's safe landing net
     I'm peacefully asleep,
     That in His mercy I'll be judged
     As good enough to keep."

     Jesus said, *"..Follow Me, and I will make you fishers of men."*
     (Matthew 4:19.)

167. Over 600 years ago Thomas A. Kempis wrote these words:

"If thou knowest the whole Bible by heart, and the sayings of all the philosophers, what would it profit thee without the love of God and without grace?"

2 Corinthians 13:14, *"The grace of the Lord Jesus Christ, and the love of God, and the communion of the Holy Spirit be with you all. Amen."*

168. "Like a piano, you may not be GRAND but you can be UPRIGHT."

Psalm 32:11, *"Be glad in the Lord and rejoice, you righteous; and shout for joy, all you upright in heart!"*

169. Sam had received a pocket-knife for his birthday. He took it to school to show his friends.

As it passed from hand to hand, one said, "It's a beautiful knife", another, "It's got four blades", another, "It's bright red" yet another, "It's sharp".

Then the owner said, "But best of all it's mine!"

David the Psalmist could say, *"The Lord is MY shepherd."* (Psalm 23:1).

170. A group of men were having a discussion as to the value of various translations of the Bible.

One of the young men, who had been silent for quite a while, said, "I prefer my mother's version to any other. She has translated it into the language of daily life for me ever since I was old enough to understand it."

2 Corinthians 3:3, *"You are manifestly an epistle of Christ, ministered by us, written not with ink but by the Spirit of the living God, not on tablets of stone but on tablets of flesh, that is, of the heart."*

171. Each evening a mother read to her son from "Pilgrim's Progress". Nearing the end of the book the boy asked his mother which of the characters she liked best. She replied, "Christian, of course; he is the hero of the story."

The boy said, "I like Christiana best, because when Christian set out on his pilgrimage he went alone; but Christiana took the children with her."

Jesus said, *"Let the little children come to Me, and do not forbid them; for of such is the kingdom of God."* (Mark 10:14).

172. You have heard the words, "Our extremity is God's opportunity".

A young lad had been shut in a room by himself as a punishment for bad conduct. He was overheard to pray, "O God, now is Your chance to make me a good boy."

Psalm 51:10, "Create in me a clean heart, O God, and renew a steadfast spirit within me."

173. A person once said, "I should have been proud to have held the spy-glass for Columbus, to have picked up the fallen brush for Michael Angelo, to have carried Milton's bag, to have blacked Shakespeare's boots, or to have blown the bellows for Handel."
Colossians 3:23, *"And whatever you do, do it heartily, as to the Lord and not to men."*

174. An interesting story is told of a Sunday school teacher who was showing her class the well-known picture of the "Mother's of Salem".

In the picture one saw some of the mothers pushing their children towards the Saviour. The teacher asked, "Do you like the picture? Is there any part that you do not understand?"

One little lad walked to the picture, and laying his finger on a little one who was being pushed along to Jesus asked, "Why does he need to be driven to the Saviour? He should go without pushing when Jesus invited him."

Song of Solomon 1:4, *"Lead me away! We will run after you"*

175. Did you know that, Cleopatra's Needle was brought to London in 1878, and set up on the Thames Embankment, and that a number of articles were deposited in a cavity underneath.?
Perhaps you did. But did you know that amongst these articles were translations of John 3:16 in 215 languages?

"For God so loved the world that He gave His only begotten Son, that whoever believes in Him should not perish but have everlasting life."

176. Did you hear of a child of six who had been introduced into the company of a group of dignified clergymen? He was offered an orange if he could tell them where God was.

The bright little lad said, "Tell me where He is not, and I will give you two!"

Psalm 139:7-12, *"Where can I go from your Spirit? Or where can I flee from your presence? If I ascend to heaven, You are there; If I make my bed in hell, behold, You are there...the darkness and the light are both alike to You."*

177.   If I had been asked some years ago as to how many hairs the average man or woman has on their head I would have said around 3,000.

But I have since learnt that there are 100,000 hairs!
Luke 12:7, *"But the very hairs of your head are all numbered. Do not fear therefore; you are of more value than many sparrows."*

178.   I once read the story of an elderly minister who on his retirement received from the congregation a cheque, a clock and a specially inscribed Bible.

After the minister and his wife had settled down in their new home they received a visit from an elder of the church. Seeing the Bible lying on the table he opened it just to refresh his memory of the inscription they had placed in it.

The minister had added at the bottom these words: "The cheque has gone, the clock is going, but the Word of the Lord abideth for ever."

1 Peter 1:23, *"Having been born again, not of corruptible seed but incorruptible, through the Word of God which lives and abides for ever."*

179.   To the young and single, consider these words very carefully:

"Marriage is either a holy wedlock or an unholy deadlock."

2 Corinthians 6:14, *"Do not be unequally yoked with unbelievers, for what fellowship has righteousness with lawlessness? And what communion has light with darkness?".*

180.   How true are these words:

"The love in your heart
  Wasn't put there to stay.
For love isn't love
  'Till you give it away."

Remember, the love we give is the only love we keep!

1 John 4:7, *"Beloved, let us love one another, for love is of God; and everyone who loves is born of God and knows God."*

181.   Did you know that the adult human body contains approximately 650 muscles, over 100 joints, 100,000 km of blood vessels and 13,000 million nerve cells?

Psalm 139:14, *"I will praise You, for I am fearfully and wonderfully made."*

182. Speaking on happiness one has said, "Happiness is like manna. It is to be gathered and enjoyed every day; it will not keep; it cannot be accumulated; nor need we go out of ourselves or into remote places to gather it, since it is rained down from heaven at our doors, or rather within them"
Psalm 144:15, *"Happy are the people who are in such a state: happy are the people whose God is the Lord!"*

183. Here is one for preachers:

    "The Word without the Spirit - Dry up!
    The Spirit without the Word - Blow up!
    The Word and the Spirit - Grow up!"

    2 Peter 3:18, *"But grow in the grace and knowledge of our Lord and Saviour Jesus Christ.."*

184. Take time to consider this thought: "The texture of eternity is woven on the looms of time."

    Ecclesiastes 7:2, *"It is better to go to the house of mourning than to go to the house of feasting. For that is the end of all men; and the living will take it to heart."*

185. Benjamin Franklin wrote: "The best thing to give to an enemy is forgiveness; to an opponent tolerance; to a friend, your ear; to your child, good example; to your father, reverence; to your mother conduct that will make her proud of you; to yourself, respect; to all, charity."

    1 Corinthians 13:13, *"And now abide faith, hope, love, these three; but the greatest of these is love."*

186. Here is a five second sermon: "It wasn't raining when Noah built the ark."

    Hebrews 11:7, *"By faith Noah, being divinely warned of things not yet seen, moved with godly fear, prepared an ark for the saving of his household, by which he condemned the world, and became heir of the righteousness which is according to faith."*

187. Which counter do you go to? "Some people spend most of their life at the complaint counter"
1 Thessalonians 5:12-13, *"And we urge you, brethren, to recognize those who labour among you, and are over you in the Lord and admonish you. And to esteem them very highly in love for their work's sake. Be at peace among yourselves."*

188. Dr.J.H.Jowett on one occasion said, "The real measure of our wealth is how much we should be worth if we lost all our money."

Matthew 6:20, *"But lay up for yourselves treasures in heaven, where neither moth and rust destroys and where thieves do not break in and steal."*

189. A little fellow once asked, "Why is it that God puts vitamins in cod liver oil and spinach and not in chewing gum and lemonade?"

Hebrews 12:11, *"Now no chastening seems to be joyful for the present, but grievous; nevertheless, afterwards it yields the peaceable fruit of righteousness to those who have been trained by it."*

190. Here is something worth remembering: "Religion was meant to be our steering wheel - not our spare wheel."

James 1:27, *"Pure and undefiled religion before God and the Father is this: to visit orphans and widow in their trouble, and to keep oneself unspotted from the world."*

191. Take note: "Silence can be valuable: don't break it unless you can improve on it."

Isaiah 53:7, *"He was oppressed and He was afflicted, yet He opened not His mouth; He was led as a lamb to the slaughter, and as a sheep before its shearers is silent."*

192. Little Albert was one day turning over the leaves of the dusty family Bible when suddenly he turned to his mother and said: "Mam, is this God's Book?" "Yes!"
"Why, then," said Albert, "hadn't we better send it back to God, for we never use it?"

Matthew 22:29, *"Jesus answered and said to them, 'You are mistaken, not knowing the Scriptures nor the power of God.'"*

193. Here is a wonderful truth on forgiveness: A young blind lad was asked what forgiveness was. He answered, "It is the fragrance that flowers breathe when trampled upon."

Luke 23:34, *"Then Jesus said, 'Father, forgive them for they do not know what they do....'"*

194. Here are the words of the famous American millionaire, Vanderbilt:

"Such wealth as mine is too heavy a burden for any man to bear. The weight of it is crushing me and killing me. I have no pleasure in it, and no use for it."

Psalm 32:1, *"Blessed is he whose transgression is forgiven, whose sin is covered."*

195. There are some questions to which we cannot find an answer. For example, "Where does the fire go to when it goes out?" Or, "Where does your lap go to when you stand up?"

Little Lois coming home from school asked her mother, "Where do the strokes made on the blackboard go when rubbed out?" The mother replied, "They disappear".
Not satisfied, Lois continued, "But where do they disappear to?"
"They vanish" replied the mother. Once more,
"But where do they vanish to?"
"The only thing I can say," says the mother, "They are blotted out."

Hebrews 10:17, *"...their sins and their lawless deeds I will remember no more."*

196. It has been said that "The Bible is a loaf, every chapter is a slice, every verse a bite."

John 6:58, *"This is the bread which came down from heaven - not as your fathers ate the manna, and are dead. He who eats this bread will live for ever."*

197. After hearing a sermon on "Mary and Martha" a certain doctor was asked which of the two sisters he would have preferred for a wife.

He replied, "I should like Martha before dinner and Mary after dinner."

Ephesians 4:7, *"But to each of us grace was given according to the measure of Christ's gift."*

198. An interesting story is told of an Indian spy who had rendered valuable assistance to the United States Government during the Civil War.

He was rewarded by a certificate which entitled him to an annual pension. Considering the certificate as a kind of charm, he put a string through it, and wore it round his neck for as long as he lived! He never drew a dollar of his pension!

John 1:12, *"But as many as RECEIVED Him, to them He gave the right to become children of God, even to those who believe in His name."*

199. A wee Scottish lassie, on being asked by her Sunday school teacher, "What is patience?" replied, "Wait a wee and dinna weary."

James 1:4, *"But let patience have its perfect work, that you may be perfect and complete, lacking nothing."*

200. Is it not true that "If you aim for nothing, you're sure to hit it?"

Daniel 1:8, *"But Daniel purposed in his heart that he would not defile himself with the portion of the king's delicacies.."*

201. Here is sound advice: "The best way to break a bad habit is to drop it."

Ecclesiastes 3:1, *"To everything there is a season, a time for every purpose under heaven."*

202. C.A.Coulson says, "A denial of God is practically always the result of shutting one eye. It may be for this reason that God gave us two."

Matthew 10:33, *"but whoever denies Me before men, him I will also deny before My Father Who is in heaven."*

203. One night Bishop William Quayle found it very difficult to sleep so be began pacing his bedroom. The story goes on to say that God said to him:

"Quayle, you go to bed, I'll sit up the rest of the night!"

Psalm 121:4, *"Behold, He Who keeps Israel shall neither slumber nor sleep."*

204. I quote the words of Albert George Butzer, "Some Christians are not only like salt that has lost its savour, but like pepper that has lost its pep."

1 Corinthians 15:58, *"Therefore, my beloved brethren, be steadfast, immovable, always abounding in the work of the Lord, knowing that your labour is not in vain in the Lord."*

205. I once came across these words by Dale Carnegie:
"You can make more friends in two months by becoming interested in other people than you can in two years by trying to get other people interested in you."

John 15:13, *"Greater love has no one than this, that he lay down his life for his friends."*

206. Good advice: "Don't pretend to be what you don't intend to be."

Matthew 23:23, *"Woe to you, scribes and Pharisees, hypocrites! For you pay tithe of mint and anise and cumin, and have neglected the weightier matters of the law...."*

207. Looking at one of Turner's master-pieces, a lady said to him, "I never saw such colours in nature."

"No, madam," he replied, "but don't you wish you could?"

1 Corinthians 2:14, *"But the natural man does not receive the things of the Spirit of God, for they are foolishness to him; nor can he know them, because they are spiritually discerned."*

208. Give heed to these words:

    "Worry never robs tomorrow of its sorrow, it only robs today of its strength."

    Psalm 90:15, *"Make us glad according to the days in which you have afflicted us. And the years in which we have seen evil."*

209. Martin Luther once said, "A lie is like a snowball: the further you roll it, the bigger it gets."

    Colossians 3:9, *"Do not lie to one another, since you have put off the old man with his deeds."*

210. A certain gentleman who was not satisfied with his present job applied to another company that offered better wages.

    When asked for references he said, "Yes, I have two. One from my minister and one from the superintendent of my Sunday school."

    "Great" replied the manager of the company," but have you any from people who know you on week days?"

    2 Corinthians 3:2, *"You are our epistle, written in our hearts, known and read by all men."*

211. A pause for thought: "If you want to help someone to climb a hill you do not stand below and push him - you go first and stretch out a helping hand."

    Writes the apostle Paul, *"Therefore I urge you, imitate me."* (1 Corinthians 4:16).

212. Here is common sense (which is not so common today):

    "The way man wishes to go, thither his feet will carry him."

    Matthew 6:21, *"For where your treasure is, there your heart will be also."*

213. Take note: "Our children are watching: What we are, speaks louder than what we say."

    Proverbs 31:28, *"Her children rise up and call her blessed.."*

214. It has been said that, "He who puts God first will find God with him at the last!"

    Matthew 6:33, *"But seek ye first the kingdom of God and His righteousness, and all these things shall be added to you."*

215. CH..CH means NOTHING unless UR in it!"

Hebrews 10:25, *"Not forsaking the assembling of ourselves together as is the manner of some.."*

216. You will have heard the expression, "For want of a nail". I quote Benjamin Franklin:- "For want of a nail, the shoe is lost; for want of a shoe, the horse is lost; for want of a horse the rider is lost."

A little neglect may breed mischief; e.g. the tyres of your car, the frayed cable to your electric kettle, but *"How shall we escape if we neglect and refuse to pay attention to such a great salvation?"* (Heb.2:3).

217. A little girl in Sunday School misquoted 1 Timothy 1:15 and said, "Christ Jesus came into the world to save cinders"

But how true! He takes the cinders, clinkers, the ashes, the burnt-out hopeless lives, and transforms them and makes them glorious and new.

"For if a man is in Christ he becomes a new person altogether." (2 Cor.5:17).

219. In these few lines taken from the Bible there is medical therapy that would prevent millions of cases of mental illness:

> "Come, listen to me, my sons,
>   I will teach you true religion.
> 'Tis your desire to live,
>   To live long and be happy?
> Then keep your tongue from evil,
>   keep your lips from deceit;
> shun evil and do good,
>   seek to be friendly - aim at that" (Psa.34:11-14).

220. Some years ago a well-known Scottish preacher was addressing a large gathering of boys in Glasgow. After telling them an interesting story, he said, "Now boys, the moral of the story is," when a young ragamuffin cried out, "Never mind the moral, Sir, gi'e us another story"

The Bible is His Story. It is the His-tory of Jesus Christ. (Jn.3:16).

221. It has been said that "As to a very rich man, a thousand sovereigns are as one penny, to the eternal God a thousand years are as one day."

"For a thousand years in Your sight are but as yesterday when it is past, and as a watch in the night." (Psa. 90:4). The apostle Peter says similar words, "Nevertheless do not let this fact escape you, beloved, that with the Lord one day is as a thousand years, and a thousand years as one day." (2 Pet.3:8).

222. A friend of mine, Ian MacPherson, wrote, "The bitterest cup with

Christ is better than the sweetest cup without Him."

Psalm 16:6, *"You, O Lord, are the portion of my inheritance and my cup; you maintain my lot."*

223. Wrote George Davis, "The probability of life originating by accident is comparable to the probability of the complete dictionary resulting from an explosion in a printing factory."

Isaiah 42:5, *"Thus says God the Lord, Who created the heavens and stretched them out, Who spread forth the earth and that which comes from it."*

224. Here is a Chinese proverb: " You cannot prevent the birds of sadness from flying over your head, but you can prevent them building nests in your hair."

Speaking of the mustard seed, *"which indeed is the least of all the seeds; but when it is grown it is greater than the herbs and becomes a tree, so that the birds of the air come and nest in its branches."*

(Matthew 13:32).

225. Consider this verse from a well-known song:

"Could we with ink the ocean fill,
   And were the sky of parchment made,
Were every blade of grass a quill,
   And every man a scribe by trade;
To write the love of God above,
   Would drain that ocean dry;
Nor would the scroll contain the whole,
   Tho' stretched from sky to sky."

John 3:16, *"For God so loved the world that He gave His only begotten Son, that whoever believes in Him should not perish but have everlasting life."*

226. A lady opened a pot of jam to discover a small piece of wood inside. She wrote to the manufacturers about it.

She received the following reply, "Dear Madam, please note that on the label it says "branches everywhere!"

1 Thessalonians 1:8, *"For from you the word of the Lord has sounded forth, not only in Macedonia and Achaia, but also in every place..."*

227. Speaking of the Bible, writes A.T.Pierson, "While other books inform,

and some few reform, this book transforms."

2 Timothy 3:15, *"And that from childhood you have known the Holy Scriptures, which are able to make you wise for salvation through faith which is in Christ Jesus."*

228. "It is nice to be important, but much more important to be nice."

Ephesians 4:32, *"And be kind to one another, tender-hearted, forgiving one another, just as God in Christ also forgave you."*

229. James was telling his pals, "My mother goes to bingo because she often wins something she wants."

"Oh" says Sid, "My mother never goes to the bingo. She has me and my little twin brothers and she says that's all she wants!"

1 Tim.6:8, *"And having food and clothing, with these we shall be content."*

230. Take this in: "It is better to swallow angry words than to have to eat them afterwards."

Proverbs 16:32, *"He who is slow to anger is better than the mighty, and he who rules his spirit than he who takes a city."*

231. The Jewish Fathers say: There are four characters of scholars:

Quick to hear and quick to forget: his gain is cancelled by his loss. Slow to hear and slow to forget: his loss is cancelled by his gain. Quick to hear and slow to forget: He is wise. Slow to hear and quick to forget: this is an evil lot.

James 1:19, *"..Let every man be quick to hear, (a ready listener), slow to speak, slow to take offence and to get angry."*

232. A daughter once heard her dear old mother praying, and in so doing misquoted Psalm 46:1, "God is our refuge and strength, a very present help in trouble."

She prayed, "O God, our very PLEASANT help in trouble." Yet how true! He is able to bring pleasantness even into our troubles.

Of heavenly wisdom it is said, *"Her ways are ways of pleasantness,and all her paths are peace."* (Proverbs 3:17).

233. It has been said that "For every minute you are angry, you loose 60 seconds of happiness."

Psalm 37:8, *"Cease from anger, and forsake wrath; do not fret - it only causes harm."*

234. Watch out! "People who fly into a rage always make a bad landing"

says Will Roger.

Ecclesiastes 7:9, *"Do not hasten in your spirit to be angry, for anger rests in the bosom of fools."*

235.   I read an interesting story of a hunter who kept on getting lost in the forests. His friend advised him to buy a compass. On his next trip he got lost yet again and lay out all night.

When asked why he did not use the compass he replied, "I did, but I could not make the needle point to the North, it would only point South-West."

For the same reason many fail to get the right direction in life because they are afraid to take the Bible and go in the direction it points.

Psalm 23:3, *"he leadeth me in the paths of righteousness."*

236.   You have all heard of a leap year. "Leap year coming once in four, February then has one day more."

But have you heard of a "leap second"? If not, just a second and I'll tell you.

To keep clock time in line with astronomical time the clocks around the world were turned back by one second at midnight Greenwich Mean Time on the lst July 1983, this being the 11th such leap second to be introduced to the calendar since 1972.

The Psalmist could say, *"My times are in your Hands.."* (Psalm 31:15).

237.   Many may ask, "What's in a name?"

In the Book of Genesis 25:14 we have the names of three of Ishmael's sons - Mishma, Dumah and Masse. They mean "hear", "keep silence", and "bear."

Many centuries later James, the apostle, penned the following words: *"...be swift to hear, slow to speak, slow to wrath."!* (James 1:19).

238.   A wayward boy wandered from home, spending days and nights in riotous living. Coming to the end of himself he wrote home to his mother asking for forgiveness, and if he could return.
He told her that on a certain one day he would pass the old home and if he saw a while sheet on the clothes line he would take it as a sign he would be welcomed.
Mother-like she gathered up every white sheet in the house and hung them on the ropes!
Isaiah 55:7, "Let the wicked forsake his way, and the unrighteous man his thoughts; let him return to the Lord. And He will have mercy on him; and to our God, for He will abundantly pardon."

239.   Every musical string is musical because it is tied at both ends, and

must vibrate within a limited measure of space.

Cut the string and let it fly loose and it no more gives out music. It is free, but useless.

Psalm 33:2, *"Praise the Lord with the harp; make medody to Him with an instrument of ten strings."*

240. Rastus had been actually caught inside a hen-house. He appeared in the local court, where he flatly denied being there for the purpose of abstracting chickens.

"Yes, but look here, Rastus," said the magistrate, "if you were not going to steal chickens, what on earth were you doing in that coop?"

And then Rastus, with monumental ingenuousness, and without the flicker of an eyelid, replied: "Jedge, ah was jest a-testin' ma will-power!"

Proverbs 4:14-15, *"Do not enter the path of the wicked, and do not walk in the way of evil. Avoid it, do not travel on it; turn away from it and pass on."*

241. Consider the power of words:
> "A careless word may kindle strife;
> A cruel word may wreck a life.
> A bitter word may hate instil;
> A brutal word may smite and kill.
> A gracious word may smooth the way;
> A joyous word may light the day.
> A timely word may lessen stress;
> A loving word may heal and bless."

Psalm 19:14, *"Let the words of my mouth and the meditation of my heart be acceptable in Your sight, O Lord, my strength and my redeemer."*

242. Here is a Hindu legend:

It says that long ago a much tempted man went to his king, and said, "O King, how can I resist temptation?"

The king replied, "Take a full pitcher of water and go through the crowded streets of my city. Go through the part where the great fair is being held. Two of my soldiers shall go with you, with naked swords. If you spill one drop of water they will kill you, but if you return to the palace with the water unspilled, I will tell you the answer to your question." The man did as commanded, and returned with the water unspilled.

"Did you not see the pleasures of the fair, the dancing crowds and all the attractions that are there?" the king asked him.

The man replied, "Sire, my eyes did see nothing else but the water. If I had looked elsewhere it would have been spilled. I saw and thought of nothing else."

"As you fixed your eyes upon the water," said the king, "now fix them upon God; then you will not be tempted to sin."

Hebrews 12:2, "Looking unto Jesus, the Author and finisher of our faith..."

243.   "There are none so deaf as the person who refuses to hear"

Jeremiah 5:21, "Here this now, O foolish people, without understanding, who have eyes and see not, and who have ears and hear not."

244.   The Rev. Simon Smith is not too popular with many of his people, as his shortest sermons are over half-an-hour in length, and rarely, if ever, engrossingly interesting.

On a recent Monday, when on the street, he met one of his flock, and remarked, "I didn't see you in church last night."

"You didn't," replied the man. "It was too wet."

"But it's always dry inside." said Mr. Smith.

"I know," said the absentee, "and that was my other reason for not being there!"

John 6:63, "It is the Spirit who gives life; the flesh profits nothing. The words that I speak to you are spirit, and they are life."

245.   Many years ago the following story was told:

Coming to a small town to be pastor of his first church, the enthusiastic clergyman was met with the flat statement that he was wasting his time, that the church was dead.

Finally, in desperation, he placed a notice in the local paper that since the church was dead, the funeral would be held the next Sunday afternoon.

The church was crowded by the curious who were rewarded by the sight of a huge coffin covered with flowers. After reading the obituary, the minister invited the people to pay their last respects.

As the long queue passed by, each looked into the coffin then glanced guiltily away. In the bottom of the coffin lay a mirror, solemnly reflecting the startled faces of the congregation."

Revelation 3:1, "...I know your works, that you have a name that you are alive, but you are dead."

246. F.B.Meyer said, "Christians are either Bibles or libels, depending on what they put first in their lives."

Luke 12:29-31, *"And do not seek what you should eat..drink..But seek the kingdom of God...."*

247. The Jews divide men into four classes:
   1. THE JUST who said: What is mine is mine; what is thine is thine.
   2. THE ACCOMMODATING who said: What is mine is thine; what is thine is mine.
   3. THE PIOUS who said: What is mine is thine; what is mine let it be thine.
   4. THE UNGODLY who said: What is mine is mine; what is thine shall be mine.

Romans 5:6, *"For when we were yet without strength, in due time Christ died for the ungodly."*

248. When the visiting preacher was asked if he would like any particular hymn to be sung to agree with his sermon replied, "No, no, as a matter of fact, I hardly ever know what I am going to say until I arrive in the pulpit."

"Oh, well, in that case," said the vicar, "Perhaps we had better have the hymn, 'For those...at sea!'"

2 Timothy 2:15, *"Be diligent to present yourself approved to God, a worker who does not need to be ashamed, rightly dividing the word of truth."*

249. An eminent surgeon worked on the eyes of a little girl who had been blind from birth. The operation had been successful. As the final bandage fell off the little girl flew into her mother's arms - "Oh Mummy, why didn't you tell me it was so beautiful?"

The mother replied, "My precious child, I tried to tell you, but I couldn't do it!"

1 Corinthians 2:9, *"But it is written: 'Eye has not seen, nor ear heard, nor have entered into the heart of man the things which God has prepared for those who love Him.'"*

250. Matthew Henry once wrote, "The flower of youth never appears more beautiful than when it bends towards the Son of Righteousness."

2 Timothy 3:15, *"And that from childhood you have known the Holy Scriptures, which are able to make you wise for salvation through faith which is in Christ Jesus.".*

251. Here is a Chinese proverb: "He who stands still in the mud sticks to it."

Philippians 3:14, *"I press towards the goal for the prize of the upward call of God in Christ Jesus."*

252. Says Abraham Lincoln, "I can see how it might be possible to look down upon the earth and be an atheist, but I cannot conceive how he could look into the heavens and say there is no God."

Psalm 19:1, *"The heavens declare the glory of God; and the firmament shows His handiwork."*

253. Notice outside a church: "Wanted - workers for God - plenty of overtime."

Matthew 9:37, *"Then He (Jesus) said to His disciples, 'The harvest truly is plentiful, but the labourers are few."*

254. Robert Jones Burdette wrote, "There are two days in the week upon which and about which I never worry, two carefree days, kept sacredly free from fear and apprehension. One of these days is Yesterday, and the other is Tomorrow."

Matthew 6:34, *"Therefore do not worry about tomorrow, for tomorrow will worry about its own things. Sufficient for the day is its own trouble."*

255. It has been said, "Swallowing your pride will never give you indigestion."

Proverbs 16:19, *"Better to be of a humble spirit with the lowly, than to divide the spoil with the proud."*

256. A car stalled outside a church. The driver was tinkering with the engine with no success. He was about to express himself forcibly when His friend pointed to a Wayside Pulpit board.

It read: "Keep your temper: Nobody wants it."

Proverbs 29:22, *"An angry man stirs up strife, and a furious man abounds in transgression."*

257. The story is told of the centipede who laid down in the road and gave

up trying to walk. It was afraid in case it used the wrong foot first and tripped over, so it didn't use any of it's feet at all!

If you keep God's word, *"Then you will walk safely in your way, and your foot will not stumble."* (Proverbs 3:23).

258. Grandma was sitting on a low window-still outside her cottage reading her Bible. One young lad said to the other as they were passing by, "What is she doing?"

"Sshh," replied the other, "she is swatting for her finals!"

2 Cor.5:10, *"For we must all appear before the judgment seat of Christ, that each one may receive the things done in the body, according to what he has done, whether good or bad."*

259. "This world is a bridge. Pass over it, but do not build a house on it" is sound advice.

Hebrews 11:9-10, *"By faith he (Abraham) sojourned in the land...for he waited for the city which has foundations, whose builder and maker is God."*

260. All is in order to "Ask God's blessing on your work, but don't expect Him to do it for you."

Philippians 2:12-13, *"....work out your own salvation with fear and trembling; for it is God Who works in you both to will and to work on behalf of His good pleasure."*

261. An interesting truth: "A cup brimful of sweet water cannot spill even one drop of bitter water however suddenly jolted."

Psalm 23:5, *"...You anoint my head with oil; my cup runs over."*

262. In a world full of voices "to hear God's voice, turn down the world's volume."

1 Samuel 3:10, *"Then the Lord came and stood and called as at other times, 'Samuel! Samuel!' And Samuel answered, 'Speak, for your servant hears.'"*

263. Did you know that the nearest stars beyond the Sun are those of Alpha Centauri system? And that they are more than four light years away?

Travelling at 55 miles an hour (88km) it would take 52 million years to reach Alpha Centauri!

Job 22:12, *"Is not God in the height of heaven? And see the highest stars, how lofty they are!"*

264. Absolutely true, "The way to better your lot is to do a lot better."

Hebrews 10:24, *"And let us consider one another in order to stir up love and good works."*

265. Horatio Bottomley, the British journalist and member of Parliament was jailed for fraud in 1922. The story goes that he preserved his wit even in prison.

It is said that a passing prison visitor, noticing him stitching mailbags, said, "Oh, Bottomley, sewing?"

"No, sir," Bottomley replied, "reaping."

Galatians 6:7, *"Do not be deceived, God is not mocked; for whatever a man sows, that he will also reap."*

266. Its a fact that "there is only a slight difference between keeping your chin up and sticking your neck out, but its worth knowing."

1 Corinthians 14:20, *"...do not be children in understanding; however, in malice be babes but in understanding be mature."*

267. And old Chinese proverb says, " We are all cast in the same mould, only some are mouldier than others!"

Romans 3:23, *"For all have sinned and fall short of the glory of God."*

268. There is an old saying, "If some folk had what some folk haven't they'd be mighty thankful for what they've gotten!"

1 Timothy 6:8, *" And having food and clothing, with these we shall be content."*

269. What do you think of this for good arithmetic: "Happiness adds and multiplies as we divide it with others."

Read the account in Mark 6:30 to 44. After all had been fed they still had *"twelve baskets full of the fragments and of the fish!"*

270. As we travel through life remember this: "Our days are identical suitcases - all the same size - but some people can pack more into them than others."

Here is an example of such a one: The apostle Paul. 2 Corinthians 11:23, *"Are you ministers of Christ? - I speak as a fool - I am more: in labours more abundant, in stripes above measure, in prisons more frequently, in deaths often.. ..."*

271. It is good to know that "no cloud comes into our life but God has put a rainbow in it!"

    Genesis 9:16, *"The rainbow shall be in the cloud, and I will look on it to remember the everlasting covenant between God and every living creature of all flesh that is on the earth."*

272. Let us never forget that no person is poor who is heir to all the riches of God.

    James 2:5, *"Listen, my beloved brethren: Has not God chosen the poor of this world to be rich in faith and heirs of the kingdom which He promised to those who love HIM?"*

273. The Scottish poet, Robert Burns wrote:

    "O wad some power the giftie gie us
    To see oursels as ithers see us."

    1 Corinthians 11:28, *"But let a man examine himself.."*

274. Wee Jock who sat at the table with his grandfather during a meal time wanted to say something to him. His grandfather reminded him that "Children should be seen and not heard." That should he have anything to say he could say it after the meal was over.

    The wee lad kept silence until the meal was completed. Then his grandfather asked him what he wanted to say. The lad replied, "It doesn't matter now, Grandad," "I was going to tell you that there was a caterpillar in your salad, but you've eaten it now!"

    Mark 13:33, *"Take heed, watch and pray; for you do not know when the time is."*

275. Take this into account: "Better than counting your years is to make your years count."

    Revelation 2:10, *"...Be faithful until death, and I will give you the crown of life."*

276. Mark Twain wrote; "When some men discharge an obligation, you can hear this discharge for miles around."

    1 Corinthians 13:1, *"Though I speak with the tongues of men and of angels, but have not love, I have become as sounding brass or a clanging cymbal."*

277. Someone wrote, "Still water and still religion freeze the quickest."

That is why the apostle Peter wrote: *"You also, as living stones, are being built up as a spiritual house..."* (1 Peter 2:5)

278. A timely word: "The best thing about the future is that it comes one day at a time."

Psalm 37:23, *"The steps of a good man are ordered by the Lord, and he delights in His way."*

279. A minister gathered his congregation together and suggested the idea of hoisting a flag from the church tower on special occasions.

A short while later one of his elderly members brought him a colourful flag. It was accepted, and one day it flew from the tower.

Shortly afterwards the minister heard a knock on his door. There was a sailor with a smile on his face. He saluted the minister and said with a large grin, "Maybe you do not know it, sir, but there's a signal flying from your church tower."

The minister looked puzzled. "What do you mean?" he asked. In answer the sailor informed him that the flag meant "In great difficulties - urgently need pilot!"

Luke 6:39, *"And He spoke a parable to them: ' Can the blind lead the blind? Will they not both fall into the ditch?'"*

280. Students, remember that "When you study the Scriptures, 'hit or miss', you're likely to miss more than you hit."

Acts 17:11, *"These were more fair-minded...they received the word with all readiness, and searched the Scriptures daily to find out whether these things were so."*

281. Observe, "Anxiety never strengthens you for tomorrow; it only weakens you for today."

Luke 12:29, *"And do not seek what you should eat or what you should drink, nor have anxious mind."*

282. How wise are these words: "We learn good things of life at our mother's knee, and the bad things at the other joints!"

Psalm 1:1, *"Blessed is the man who walks not in the counsel of the ungodly, nor stands in the path of sinners, nor sits in the seat of the scornful."*

283. Rest assured that "When God measures a man He puts the tape around the heart, not the head."

    Proverbs 4:23, *"Keep your heart with all diligence, for out of it springs the issues of life."*

284. A gentleman walking by observed an umbrella repairer at work by the road-side. He commented on the excellency of his work.

    In reply the repairer said, "I endeavour always to do a good job."

    The gentleman continued, "I expect it pays you to do that, for when your return the next time."

    The repairer answered, "It's not just that. I may never come this way again, but if I do a good job I will make it easier for the next person who comes along in my profession."

    Hebrews 13:21, *"Make you complete in every good work to do His will, working in you what is well pleasing in His sight.."*

285. I saw printed on a large wooden spoon these words: "The world's greatest stirrer."

    Proverbs 10:12, *"Hatred stirs up strife, but love covers all sins."*

286. In answer to a distress signal the life boat was launched. One of the younger members of the crew suddenly lost his nerve and felt afraid to face the fierce storm.

    He cried out - "We'll never make it back!" The skipper of the boat shouted out above the sound of the wind and waves, "We don't have to go back, but we do have to go out!"

    Mark 16:15, *"...Go into all the world and preach the gospel to every creature."*

287. I recall my mother often saying, "What's worth doing, is worth doing well."

    Luke 19:17, *"...Well done, good servant; because you were faithful in a very little, have authority over ten cities."*

288. "A pat on the back is all right provided it is administered early enough, hard enough, and low enough."

    Proverbs 22:6, *"Train up a child in the way he should go, and when he is old he will not depart from it."*

289. These words were written on an ornamental mug: "It's better to remain silent and be thought a fool than to open your mouth and prove it!"

    Psalm 141:3, *"Set a guard, O Lord, over my mouth; keep watch over the door of my lips."*

290. "Every time you turn green with envy you are ripe for trouble."

    Acts 7:9, *"And the patriarchs, becoming envious, sold Joseph into Egypt. But God was with him."*

291. When little Sally was about to run off to school her father gave her a kiss on the cheek. Immediately the little girl took out her handkerchief and wiped her face.

    The father was somewhat surprised by this seeming show of bad manners. But Sally said, with a smile on her face, "It's alright Dad, I was just rubbing it in!"

    Song of Solomon 1:2, *"Let him kiss me with the kisses of his mouth - For your love is better than wine."*

292. It is said that the best exercise for the heart is to reach down and pull other people up!

    Galatians 6:2, *"Bear one another's burdens, and so fulfil the law of Christ."*

293. "Many people are lonely because they build walls instead of bridges."

    "He who finds his life will lose it, and he who loses his life for my sake will find it." (Matthew 10:39).

294. I am sure that you will agree with me when I say that a road map will tell you everything you want to know except how to fold it up again!

    The Bible is different. Listen to the words of Paul to Timothy, *"And from childhood you have known the Holy Scriptures, which are able to make you wise for salvation through faith which is in Christ Jesus."* (2 Timothy 3:15).

295. In darker moments think on this: "If you can't find a sunny side to life, polish up the darkside."

    The apostle Paul writes, *"Not that I speak in regard to need, for I have learned in whatever state I am, to be content."* (Philippians 4:11).

296. It is worth remembering that "If you remove the rocks, the brook will lose its song."

    Job in his affliction could say, *"Where is God my Maker, Who gives me songs in the night?"* (Job.35:10).

297. Young Sarah had an eye to business. One day she visited a farm and said she wanted a large water-melon.

    "That," said the farmer pointing to a large one, "will be three dollars."

    The young girl replied, "I've only got thirty five cents."

    The farmer drew her attention to a very small water melon in the field and said, "How about that one?"

    "Okay," said Sarah, "I'll take it. But leave it on in the vine. I'll be back for it in a month's time!"

    Read the parable of the growing seed in Mark 4:26-29.

298. I came across these sound words of advice many years ago:
    "Don't look for the flaws
    As you go through life,
    And even if you find 'em,
    'Tis wise and kind to be somewhat blind,
    And look for the virtues behind 'em."

    Proverbs 10:12, *"Hatred stirs up strife, but love covers all sins."*

299. Wrote Victor Alfsen, "God can do wonders with a broken heart if you give him all the pieces"

    Psalm 34:18, *"The Lord is near to those who have a broken heart, and saves such as have a contrite spirit."*

300. Someone rightly said, "Every lock of sorrow has a key of promise to fit it."

    John 16:20, *"Most assuredly, I say to you that you will weep and lament, but the world will rejoice; and you will be sorrowful, but your sorrow will be turned into joy."*

301. May these words warm your heart, "One believing heart sets another on fire."

    Luke 24:32, *"And they said to one another, 'Did not our heart burn within us while He (Jesus) talked with us on the road, and while He opened the Scriptures to us?'"*

302. I am sure you will agree that "Life without laughter is like beef without gravy."

     Psalm 126:2, *"Then our mouth was filled with laughter, and our tongues with singing..."*

303. This is worthy of consideration, "The grass may look greener next door, but it's just as hard to cut."

     Hebrews 13:5, *"Let your conduct be without covetousness, and be content with such things as you have.."*

304. Wee Jean asked for the light to be left on when she was went to bed.

     Her mother replied, "There is no need to be afraid of the dark"

     "I'm not afraid of it," said Jean, "but it gets in my eyes and I can't see anything!"
     1 Corinthians 13:12, *"For now we see in a mirror, dimly, but then face to face. Now I know in part, but then I shall know just as I also am known."*

305. Battle Abbey was built by William the Conqueror on the very field where he overcame Harold the Saxon in the battle of Hastings.

     It is said that he granted a royal privilege to the Abbot to pardon any criminal, however great his offence, if he claimed that pardon in the king's name.
     While many gladly owned their guilt and received pardon, others, because of pride, did not.

     Acts 13:38, *"Therefore let it be known to you, brethren, that through this man (Jesus) is preached to you the forgiveness of sins."*

306. Wrote W.H.G.Thomas, "In things essential, unity. In things doubtful, liberty. In all things, charity. And beneath all things, fidelity."

     Titus 2:10, *"Not pilfering, but showing all good fidelity, that they may adorn the doctrine of God our Saviour in all things."*

307. On a drinking fountain in Aberdeen there is an inscription in Gaelic: "Gaed mille failte."

     It means - "A hundred thousand welcomes."

     Revelation 22:17, *"And the Spirit and the Bride say 'Come!' And let him who hears say, 'Come!' And let him who thirsts come. And whoever desires, let him take of the water of life freely."*

308. There are many kinds of people in the world. Some are like wheel barrows - no use unless pushed!

The apostle Paul was of a different sort: *"I press towards the goal for the prize of the upward call of God in Christ Jesus."* (Philippians 3:14)

309. Being shown through a state prison in France, a royal prince had conferred on him the power to give a prisoner his freedom in honour of his visit.

Questioning various convicts, he was told that some had been falsely charged, others wrongly judged. But one grey-haired man acknowledged the justice of his sentence, declaring he got no more than he deserved.

Laying his hand on this man's shoulder, the prince said, "You are the man." And he, the worst man there, according to his own confession, was set free.
1 Timothy 1:15, *"This is a faithful saying and worthy of all acceptance, that Christ Jesus came into the world to save sinners, of whom I am chief."*

310. Have you ever considered the fact that "Happiness is a journey, not a destination?"

Psalm 146:5, *"Happy is he who has the God of Jacob for his help, whose hope is in the Lord his God."*

311. When Calais was captured by Edward III he told the conquered people that he would spare them if six of their leaders would deliver themselves with halters round their necks for execution.

St. Pierre, the French commander, offered himself, and five others quickly followed.

These men were willing to die so as to save their country men.

Romans 5:6, *"For when we were still without strength, in due time Christ died for the ungodly."*

312. A hundred tons of wheat was sold to a miller by a grain merchant. It was done from a sample of half-a-pound. The stock was accepted in the sample, and guaranteed to be the same.

1 Cor.15:20, *"But now Christ has risen from the dead, and has become the first-fruits of those who have fallen asleep."*

313. Over a century ago, Voltaire, the French infidel, sat writing a book which he said would "demolish the Bible forever." And that within a century there would not be "a Bible on the face of the earth."

Since then millions of Bible have been circulated, Voltaire's house having become the Bible Society's depot in Geneva!
Acts 12:24, *"But the word of God grew and multiplied."*

314. Take this into account. When an account is paid, the creditor blots it out of his book, and gives a receipt: it can be charged no more.

Isaiah 44:22, *"I have blotted out, like a thick cloud, your transgressions, and like a cloud, your sins..."*

315. Henry Ward Beecher wrote, "In this world it is not what we take up but what we give up that makes us rich."

Mark 10:29-30, *"Jesus answered and said,....there is no one who has left house or brothers or sisters or father or mother...for my sake and the gospel's, who shall not receive a hundredfold now in this time...and in the ages to come, eternal life."*

316. An interesting story is told of a sunburned fisherman who stood in Castlegate, Aberdeen. There, preaching to a large crowd he said in broad Doric:

"God gave His Son for naething: Christ gives away salvation for naething: an' ye can be saved jist noo, where ye stan' without gein' onything. It's a' for naething."

Isaiah 55:1, *"Ho! Everyone who thirsts, come to the waters; and you who have no money, come, buy and eat. Yes, come, buy wine and milk without money and without price."*

317. The last man who left the doomed S.S. London as it was sinking in the Bay of Biscay, on the 11th January 1866 said that the last words he heard as he took his place in a small boat was a group of passengers singing, "Rock of Ages".

Psalm 18:2, *"The Lord is my rock and my fortress and my deliverer; my God, my strength, in whom I will trust."*

318. Says Robert Cleath, "The doubter can't find God for the same reason that a thief can't find a policeman."

Psalm 53:1, *"The fool has said in his heart, 'There is no God.'"*

319. The gatekeeper had signalled all clear for the approaching train, when suddenly his little boy stepped out of the cottage door on to the line, at the side of which was a projecting rock.

His father realized that he could not reach him in time and save him from the fast approaching train.

He called out, "Fred, cling to the rock!" and the child accustomed to obey, locked his wee arms around the rough edge of the rock, and was saved.

2 Samuel 22:2-3 *"And he said, 'The Lord is my rock, my fortress and deliverer; the God of my strength, in Him I will trust."*

320.   "Envy provides the mud that failure throws at success." (Anon).

Proverbs 14:30, *"A sound heart is life to the body, but envy is rottenness to the bones."*

321.   Wrote one, "If you have your sight; you are blessed. If you have insight; you are a thousand times blessed."

Philippians 1:9, *"And this I pray, that your love may abound still more and more in knowledge and all discernment"*

322.   Many years ago the story was told of an infidel who scornfully pointed to one who had professed Christianity, and gone astray.

Dr. Mason, who was standing by, heard the remark and asked, "Did you ever hear of a scoff being raised because an infidel went astray?" The scorner admitted he had not.

"Then," replied the doctor, "you thereby admit that Christianity is a holy religion, and that its professors should be so too. Your scoff, therefore, pays the highest compliment."

James 1:27, *"Pure and undefiled religion before God and the Father is this: to visit orphans and widows in their troubles, and to keep oneself unspotted from the world."*

323.   It has been said that most of us will never do great things, but we can do some things in a great way."

Colossians 3:23, *"And whatever you do, do it heartily, as to the Lord and not to men."*

324.   As Sir Walter Scott lay dying at Abbotsford he asked his son-in-law to bring him the book.

"What book, Sir Walter?" asked Lockhart. "There is but one book - the Bible" came the reply from the dying man.

To he who had written many, some fiction and some fact, the Book of God alone was of value on the borders of Eternity.

1 Peter 1:23, *"Having been born again, not of corruptible seed but incorruptible, through the Word of God which lives and abides for ever."*

325. G.K.Chesterton said, "The evolutionist seems to know everything about the missing link except the fact that it is missing."

Romans 1:25, *"Who exchanged the truth of God for a lie, and worshipped and served the creature rather than the Creator, Who is blessed for ever. Amen."*

326. Said James Learmont: "Religion is bread for daily use, not cake for special occasions."

Matthew 6:11, *"Give us this day our daily bread."*

327. Standing on the steps of his home in Stepney, Dr. Barnardo, on a snowy night, saw a shivering boy come along to ask for admittance.

To test the lad, the doctor spoke roughly, and enquired if he had any references. Lifting up his shivering, bare blue arms, the lad replied, "Only these."

Luke 15:2, *"And the Pharisees and scribes murmured, saying, 'This man receives sinners and eats with them.'"*

328. J.I.Packer asked, "How many Christians live their lives packed up and ready to go?" Are you a packer?

Philippians 1:23, *"For I am hard pressed between the two, having a desire to depart and be with Christ, which is far better."*

329. About a century and a half ago, an infidel German Countess gave orders that her grave should be covered with a solid granite slab, with large blocks of stone clasped with iron around.

On the stone the following words were to be engraved: "This burial place must never be opened to all Eternity."

A tiny seed sprouted under the cover, shot its shoots between the slabs, grew and increased until it lifted the granite. In Hanover today this stands as God's answer to the infidel's challenge.

John 11:25, *"Jesus said to her, "I am the resurrection and the life. He who believes in Me, even though he dies, he shall live."*

330. William Henry Davies, the Welsh poet once wrote; "What is this life if, full of care, We have no time to stand and stare..."

Psalm 19:1, *"The heavens declare the glory of God; and the firmaments show his handiwork."*

331. "A Christian is not a person who has made a new start in life, but a person who has received a new life to start with" (Anon).

   2 Corinthians 5:17, *"Therefore, if anyone is in Christ, he is a new creation...all things have become new."*

332. It is good to remember that whenever you throw mud at somebody you lose ground.

   Matthew 7:3, *"And why do you look at the speck in your brother's eye, but do not consider the plank in your own eye?"*

333. Notice in Burglar Alarm shop: Ideal gift for a person who has got everything.

   Job 11:18, *"And you will be secure, because there is hope; yes, you would dig about you, and take your rest in safety."*

334. Wrote Paul Frost, "A character, no more than a fence, can be strengthened by whitewash."

   Matthew 23:27, *"Woe to you, scribes, and Pharisees, hypocrites! For you are like whitewashed tombs which indeed appear beautiful outwardly, but inside are full of dead men's bones and all uncleanness."*

335. "When you are looking for faults to correct, look in the mirror!" (Anon)

   Luke 6:41, *"And why do you look at the speck in your brother's eye, but do not perceive the plank in your own eye?"*

336. The Sunday School teacher was giving a lesson on love to a class of small children. Then she asked the question, "Why does God love us all so much?"

   One little hand shot up. "Yes?" asked the teacher. And wee Lyn replied, "Because, Miss, God has only one of each of us!"

   Matthew 18:10, *"Take heed that you do not despise one of these little ones, for I say to you that in heaven their angels always see the face of my Father Who is in heaven."*

337. Think on these words: "Christianity begins where religion ends - with the resurrection."

   1 Corinthians 15:20, "But now Christ has risen from the dead.

338.   Jeff wrote his first letter to Aunt Mabel. It was scarcely readable. His mother doubted whether the letter would ever reach his aunt.

Nevertheless his mother addressed the envelope in a neat hand and placed the blurred letter inside.

The child was delighted and danced with joy as his mother closed the envelope. He said, "It will go now, mother, because it is inside, and they will only look at the envelope."

Colossians 3:3, *"For you died, and your life is hidden with Christ in God."*

339.   I came across these words the other day, "A lot of indigestion is caused by people having to eat their own words."

Colossians 4:6, *"Let your speech always be with grace, seasoned with salt, that you may know how you ought to answer each other."*

340.   Graven on the tomb of an Eastern ruler are two fingers represented as snapping against each other, with these words below: "All is not worth that." Such was his value of the world.

Ecclesiastes 1:2, *"Vanity of vanities, says the Preacher; Vanity of vanities, all is vanity"* Paul says, *"For me to live is Christ, and to die is gain."* (Philippians 1:21).

341.   Spare a moment to think on this: "One minute of keeping your mouth shut is worth an hour of explanation."

Proverbs 21:23, *"Whosoever guards his mouth and tongue keeps his soul from troubles."*

342.   A young man said to an elderly person who was a Christian, "The Bible is out of date. We badly need a new one."

Replied the old gentleman, "I'll keep my old one till I get a better one."

John 6:68, *"Then Simon Peter answered Him, 'Lord, to whom shall we go? You have the words of eternal life.'"*

343.   Someone said, "The pure river of God will continue to flow until it empty itself into the ocean of Eternity."

Revelation 22:1, *"And he showed me a pure river of the water of life, clear as crystal, proceeding from the throne of God and of the Lamb."*

344. It is important to:
"Do what you can, being what you are,
Shine like a glow-worm if you cannot be a star.
Work like a pulley if you cannot be a crane,
Be a wheel-greaser if you cannot drive the train."

Philippians 1:11, *"Being filled with the fruits of righteousness which are by Jesus Christ, to the glory and praise of God."*

345. This is a fact, "A Bible that is falling apart usually belongs to a person who is not!"

1 Timothy 4:15, *"Meditate on these things; give yourself entirely to them, that your progress may be evident to all."*

346. Consider these words: "It is never too early to give thanks, because we don't know how soon it will be before it is too late."

"We are bound to thank God always for you, brethren, as it is fitting, because your faith grows exceedingly, and the love of every one of you all abounds towards each other." (2 Thessalonians 1:3).

347. "Our job is not to see through one another, but to see one another through."

"And if one member suffers, all the members suffer with it; or if one member is honoured, all the members rejoice with it." (1 Corinthians 12:26).

348. When out in Rhodesia (now Zimbabwe) at 5.30 each morning on the radio came five minutes on physical exercise. One morning, five minutes earlier than usual an announcer with a sense of humour said: "Here's your morning exercise, lift your little finger up and now down. Up once more, down again. Right, that's your exercise for today!"
The best exercise for the heart is to reach down and pull other people up! Gal.6:2, *"Practice bearing one another's burden, and in this way carry out the law of Christ."*

349. Walking through St. James Park one afternoon I saw an old tramp wrapped up in his rags asleep on the green.

Not an unusual sight maybe, in London. But one thing made it different. By his head was an orange. Someone must have had pity on him and left it there.

When he woke up he would know, someone cared! *"Casting all your care upon Him (God); for He careth for you."* (1 Pet.5:7).

350.   A gentleman took his typewriter to the repair shop. "I think the trouble is with one of the keys," he said.

As the repairer was taking off the cover he said: "I have seen this typewriter before, it will be the letter "I".

After examination it turned out that the letter "I" was the culprit!

Is it not the letter that causes so much trouble in our world today?" Paul said, *"..I live, yet not I, but Christ liveth in me.."* (Gal.2:20).

351.   Here is a Chinese Proverb worth remembering:

"If there is righteousness in the heart, there will be beauty in the character. If there is beauty in the character, there will be harmony in the home. If there is harmony in the home, there will be order in the nation. when there is order in the nation, there will be peace in the world."

Proverbs 14:34, *"Righteousness exalts a nation, but sin is a reproach to any people."*

352.   When you feel tempted to pass on a tale ask yourself these three questions:

1. Is it true?   2. Is it needful?   3. Is it kind?

Titus 3:1-2, *" Remind them to be subject to rulers, and authorities, to obey, to be ready for every good work, to speak evil of no one, to be peaceable, gentle, showing all humility to all men."*

353.   Mark the words of Mark Twain, "A lie can travel halfway around the world while the truth is putting on its shoes."

Psalm 40:4, *"Blessed is the man who makes the Lord his trust, and does not respect the proud, nor such as turn aside to lies."*

354.   One Christmas little Jennifer was brought to visit my elderly mother. She gazed at the picture of Jesus in Gethsemane that hung over the fire place.

At last, she asked: "Who is that gentleman?" She was told: "It's Jesus." She was silent again. Eventually she uttered, "My! Hasn't He grown."

Matthew 24:30, *"...and they shall see the Son of Man coming in the clouds of heaven with power and great glory."*

355. It is true to say that wise men still seek Christ!

John 12:21, *"Then they came to Philip, who was from Bethsaida of Galilee, and asked him, saying 'Sir, we wish to see Jesus.'"*

356. Here is a delightful story that I came across some time ago. It was about a young lad who decided to buy a Bible for his grandmother for Christmas.

Having purchased the Bible he wondered what he could write on the opening free page. He had seen some writing inside another book and decided to copy it, even though he was not sure of the meaning of the words.

When Christmas came round and grannie received her Christmas present she was delighted. Opening the Bible she saw written these words: "With the compliments and best wishes of the Author."!

Hebrews 12:2, *"Looking unto Jesus, the author and finisher of our faith, Who for the joy that was set before Him endured the cross, despising the shame, and has sat down at the right hand of the throne of God."*

357. Saw these words on a poster outside a church: "Avoid the Christmas rush. Come to church next Sunday."

Psalm 122:1, *"I was glad when they said to me, 'Let us go into the house of the Lord.'"*

358. Wrote Ironside, "There is always the danger of keeping Christmas and losing Christ".

Isaiah 7:14, *"Therefore the Lord Himself will give a sign: Behold, the virgin shall conceive and bear a Son, and shall call his name Immanuel."* (Literally, "God-With-Us").

359. Have you ever realized that Bethlehem's stable was the first step in God's love-journey to Calvary's cross?

Colossians 1:15, *"He is the image of the invisible God, the first-born over all creation."*

360. How appropriate are these words at this time of the year: "What eats you, does more harm than what you eat."

Luke 12:23 and 29, *"Life is more than food, and the body is more than clothing." "And do not seek what you should eat or what you should drink, nor have an anxious mind."*

361. An old Chinese's proverb says, "It is not how old you are, but how you are old, which matters."

Isaiah 40:31 says, *"But those who wait on the Lord shall renew their strength; they shall mount up with wings like eagles. They shall run and not be weary, they shall walk and not faint."*

362. P. Brooks once said, "Duty makes us do things well, but love makes us do them beautifully."

1 Corinthians 13:13, *"And now abide faith, hope, love, these three; but the greatest of these is love."*

363. You can rest on this: "An easy conscience makes a soft pillow."

2 Timothy 1:3, *"I thank God, whom I serve with a pure conscience, as my forefathers did, as without ceasing I remember you in my prayers night and day."*

364. The story is told of one of the greatest escape artist of all time, the famous Houdini. He did the seemingly impossible.

He was invited by the authorities to visit a jail in a small British town. It was a new jail and was announced as escape-proof. But Houdini boasted that he could get out in sixty minutes.

He was placed in a cell in the prison. But he did not get out in sixty minutes. In fact after two hours he was still trying to open the cell door!

He paused, with perspiration pouring off him - and leaned against the door. Immediately, to his surprise, it opened. The prison governor had not locked it! He had been tricked; he had tried to open a door that was open all the time.

"..see, I have set before you an open door, and no one can shut it.."
(Revelation 3:8)

365. The story is told of Dr. Guthrie, the Scottish theologian, of how one day passing through a street in Edinburgh he saw a little girl carrying a very heavy baby.

   "Lassie," he said to the little girl," surely that child is too heavy for you." "No, sir," replied the little girl, "for he is my brother."

   "Bear ye one another's burden, and so fulfil the law of Christ." (Galatians 6:2).

366. "The pleasures of sin are only for time; its wages are for eternity."

   "Choosing rather to suffer affliction with the people of God than enjoy the pleasures of sin for a season." (Hebrews 11:25).

                              * * * * *

MOORLEY'S

are growing Publishers, adding several new titles to our list each year. We also undertake private publications and commissioned works.

Our range of publications includes: **Books of Verse**
      Devotional Poetry
      Recitations
      Drama
      Bible Plays
      Sketches
      Nativity Plays
      Passiontide Plays
      Easter Plays
      Demonstrations
      Resource Books
      Assembly Material
      Songs & Musicals
      Children's Addresses
      Prayers & Graces
      Daily Readings
      Books for Speakers
      Activity Books
      Quizzes
      Puzzles
      Painting Books
      Daily Readings
      Church Stationery
      Notice Books
      Cradle Rolls
      Hymn Board Numbers

Please send a S.A.E. (approx 9" x 6") for the current catalogue or consult your local Christian Bookshop who should stock or be able to order our titles.